AMERICAN FOLK ART
THE ART OF THE COMMON MAN
IN AMERICA   1750-1900

THE MUSEUM OF MODERN ART
11 WEST 53RD STREET · NEW YORK

Reprint Edition, 1969
PUBLISHED FOR THE MUSEUM OF MODERN ART BY ARNO PRESS

The Trustees and Staff of the Museum of Modern Art wish to thank the collectors who have lent the paintings and sculptures in this exhibition. Thanks are due to Mrs. Edith Gregor Halpert for assistance in assembling the exhibition, and to Miss Elinor Robinson and Miss Dorothy Miller for assistance in compiling the catalogue notes.

AMERICAN FOLK ART

THIS exhibition represents the unconventional side of the American tradition in the fine arts. The pictures and sculptures in it are the work of craftsmen and amateurs of the eighteenth and nineteenth centuries who supplied a popular demand for art. Their makers were house painters, sign painters, portrait limners, carpenters, cabinet-makers, shipwrights, wood-carvers, stone-cutters, metal workers, blacksmiths, sailors, farmers, business men, housewives, and girls in boarding school. Many of these people had little training but all of them knew how to coordinate the activity of the hand and the eye, and had the art of making things with their hands, an art which has declined rapidly with the progress of the machine age. A good deal of their work is to be found in the older communities of the United States. It is a varied art, influenced from diverse sources, often frankly derivative, often fresh and original, and at its best an honest and straightforward expression of the spirit of a people. This work gives a living quality to the story of American beginnings in the arts, and is a chapter, intimate and quaint, in the social history of this country.

Many writers appear to have taken it for granted that the American people is not given to esthetic expression and that Puritanism is to blame for this national deficiency. The fact is that Americans have turned to art at all periods of their history. It is true that the Puritans, and the Quakers as well, were not a gay people, and that pleasing the eye was not a dominant interest with them. Yet it is a fact to be remarked that the earliest development of American art took place in the Puritan and Quaker sections. The first generations of settlers in this country were busy with the bare necessities of life and so had little time for art, but they turned to it very quickly as soon as they had won a little prosperity. There were portraits being painted in New England as early as the 1640's, and this is remarkable when we remember that even in the mother country there was no great demand for art in the seventeenth century, and that only the aristocrats and the wealthy merchants patronized the artist to any extent. All things considered it is rather surprising how quickly an American portrait school arose, and that painters as good as Robert Feke and John Singleton Copley were contemporary with the great English portrait school which began its production about the middle of the eighteenth century. The Puritans had no such aversion to art as is commonly ascribed to them. They were wedded to an austere and simple way of living, but austerity and simplicity have never been a bar to art expression in any age of the world. Paintings and carvings surviving from Puritan days, as well as thousands of craft objects, prove that they were no bar in the early days in America.

The one type of art that was not much encouraged in colonial America was religious art. The Puritan imagination was concentrated upon religion, but the iconoclastic bent of English Protestantism was against religious art, and though the early settlers often painted the walls and even the floors of their houses with landscapes and stencil designs, and had pictures on their walls, their churches and meeting-houses were severely plain. Most of the religious art which appeared in colonial America is on the tombstones of New England and in the missal illuminations and baptismal certificates of the Pennsylvania Germans.

The bulk of the material in this collection is an overflow from the crafts. American craftsmanship developed steadily and consistently from the earliest days up to the Revolution in the northern provinces, and there was a good deal more of it in the South than is generally supposed. Advertisements in news-papers of the late seventeenth and early eighteenth centuries indicate that there were many trained craftsmen in the country. Cotton Mather says that in the twelve years after the granting of a charter to the Massachusetts Bay Com-pany, "artificers to the number of some thousands" came with their families to New England. In 1678 the general court in Boston ordered the King's arms carved for the court-house "by an able artist." There are more than four hun-dred known portraits of people born in the colonies before 1701. Four hundred silversmiths are known to have worked in Boston, New York, and Philadelphia before 1800, and there were hundreds of others in Providence, Trenton, New-port, Baltimore, Charleston, and other centers throughout the country. The trade of the local silversmith flourished up to the middle of the nineteenth cen-tury, when, like most of the other crafts, it passed into the hands of the manufac-turers. The names of furniture craftsmen, men who knew how to carve, are legion. Every town had its joiners and chair makers, and various other craftsmen such as coppersmiths, braziers, and pewterers as early as the middle of the seven-teenth century.

Most of the early craftsmen were English. The culture of colonial America was basically English, though a variety of other nationalities was represented— Scotch, Welsh, Irish, Dutch, German, Swedish, and French—and these affected the English influence a good deal. Intercolonial migration changed the stock somewhat and mixed the racial strains, and this explains the variety of

4

folk art styles in certain places, such as Pennsylvania, New Jersey, New York, a few localities in Massachusetts and Maine, and in the Shenandoah Valley. Germans settled in many towns in New England and the South as well as in the German counties of Pennsylvania, and wherever they went one may expect to find characteristic examples of their folk art which is close to the peasant art of Germany.

No seventeenth century work is included in this exhibition but the seventeenth century craftsmen are mentioned here because their influence persisted in the work of the eighteenth century. The seventeenth century craftsmen in America were men who had been trained in a medieval shop tradition. This tradition in the crafts was strong in England up to the time of Inigo Jones (1573–1625), who brought in the Renaissance influence which one finds in full flower in the work of Sir Christopher Wren and Grinling Gibbons. Many American craftsmen followed the contemporary English style closely, and had the books of the English architects and designers, but there was inevitably a lag between the English and American styles, and in the rural districts the older tradition of shop practice was extremely tenacious. Local architects, house builders, carpenters, wood- and stone-carvers, and coach and sign painters preserved pre-Renaissance methods long after the professional artists had lost them, and long after they had been forgotten in Europe.

The tradition of shop practice is one of the dominant influences in the type of American art which is represented in this exhibition. Various terms have been used to describe this art, provincial, popular, folk, and primitive. Much of the work in this exhibition may be called primitive in the sense that it is the simple, unaffected and childlike expression of men and women who had little or no school training in art, and who did not even know that they were producing art. If they had been put to it they would probably have given the answer of George Hepplewhite that they were trying to "blend the useful with the agreeable." In most instances they were making things for use, such as inn and shop signs, ships' figureheads, and weather-vanes, or they had something they wanted to express and they proceeded to set down what they had to say with the means and materials at hand. While the word "primitive" might be applied to some of the material in this exhibition it has associations which make it inappropriate.

"Provincial" is not sufficiently definitive and it is not exact. Practically all American professional art up to the period of the Civil War was provincial, that is, it was a local variant of a metropolitan art the center of which was Europe.

The bulk of the examples in this exhibition are not so much local variants of a metropolitan practice as survivals of an older tradition. In the portraits, for instance, the treatment of the composition as a flat pattern, the emphasis upon outline and contour, the lack of emphasis upon modeling with light and shade, and the use of the word "limner" ("limner" is derived from "illuminer") suggest the connection between early American portraiture and manuscript illumination. The connection is there, though it is not a close one, and it has been overlaid with various other influences, such as that of the early Flemings upon English portrait painting.

"Folk art" is the most nearly exact term so far used to describe this material. It fits very well the work of such men as Joseph Pickett (No. 24), Edward Hicks (Nos. 21 and 22), John Bellamy (No. 131), and other strong personalities thrown up from the fertile plain of every-day competence in the crafts. The work of these men is folk art because it is the expression of the common people, made by them and intended for their use and enjoyment. It is not the expression of professional artists made for a small cultured class, and it has little to do with the fashionable art of its period. It does not come out of an academic tradition passed on by schools, but out of craft tradition plus the personal quality of the rare craftsman who is an artist.

Folk art, as it is defined by the objects in this exhibition, is the work of people with little book learning in art techniques, and no academic training. It does not include the work of the craftsmen who made American silver, glass, or furniture, except when their work carried over into the fine arts. The early American craftsmen could do many things. Many of the silversmiths, like Paul Revere, made engravings, and some, like Nathaniel Hurd, painted portraits. The potters of Pennsylvania made "fractur" drawings and watercolors; furniture and carriage makers, carpenters, and shipwrights carved "effigies"; blacksmiths and iron molders made weather-vanes; masons and stone-cutters carved grave-stones; house and ship painters, and coach and sign painters turned their hands to decorative paintings and portraits. Many of the early American painters began as artisans and craftsmen. Evert Duyckinck is described as a glazier, limner, and painter. Joseph Badger began as a house painter and glazier. Matthew Pratt painted signs for the tradesmen of Philadelphia. Charles Willson Peale was a saddler, silversmith, and coach and clock maker. Chester Harding was a chair maker. Edward Hicks was a carriage maker and painter. James Frothingham and John Neagle began as coach painters.

In the great periods of art the artisans and craftsmen who decorated funerary monuments, carved and painted decorations for houses and ships, and made and decorated household furniture and utensils, have been the binding element in the tradition. They have maintained the standards of craft and shop practice, helped keep alive the fundamentals of tradition in times when there were no masters, and their work has furnished the background for the development of masters. That their work was not the background for the development of American art as we know it today is one of the accidents of our art history. American sculpture, for instance, might have developed out of the tradition of the old figurehead and tombstones carvers. Our sculptors might have built on the work of the New England carvers (see Nos. 123, 124) instead of following Canova and Thorwaldsen. From the middle of the seventeenth century up to the Civil War there were in New England, New York, New Jersey, Pennsylvania, and other parts of the country, many carvers who were closer to the great tradition of their art than were the professional sculptors. William Codner, Henry Christian Geyer, and Isaac Fowle of Boston, the Lamsons of Charlestown, John Sampson of Bath, Samuel McIntire of Salem, and numerous other craftsmen could carve good portraits, and make decorative arrangements admirable for fitness, simplicity, and just proportion.

While the folk art tradition has had little to do with the development of American professional art, yet the main stream of American art was fed by the crafts during the seventeenth, eighteenth, and early nineteenth centuries. It is often hard to draw a dividing line between the art of the common man and that of the professional. Dozens of artisans and craftsmen have made their way into the ranks of the professional artists and dozens of others who did not make this happy translation are of equal merit with those who did. Folk art had a place in the life of this country from the early days of colonization up to the Civil War. After the Civil War it began to languish. The shift of economic and social forces which culminated in the war between the states was a function of the development of modern industrialism. Men and women were drawn away from the farm and from home industries into the factories. Railroads brought the rural communities closer to the cities and accelerated the urban concentration of the American people. Everywhere in the United States the machine was driving out the local craftsman. By 1865 the United States had turned the corner from a rural to an urban civilization. Machine industry was enthroned. Business enterprise made use of the limitless reproductive power of the machine to fill the land with machine-made copies of objects designed by the craftsmen whom the machine was destroying. The old gravestone cutters had been replaced by the commercial carver. The itinerant portrait painter had yielded to the photographer. The sailing ship was fading out in the brief glory of the clipper era, and steam navigation was putting the figurehead carvers out of business. In a day of almost universal literacy the carving and painting of shop signs and trade symbols became a thing of the past.

By the last quarter of the nineteenth century the craft tradition was dying, not only in America, but everywhere in the Western World. A few of the old craftsmen remained here and there, but their production was negligible and their creative efforts met with little response from a public whose taste had been trained to accept only the machine-made. By the close of the century the era of handicrafts supported by apprenticeship was definitely at an end, and American folk art was dead, except for the work of the amateur. Even in this field the output has been restricted because the American artisan in the machine age has lost his respect for hand work and has turned to avocations more in harmony with his daily life. As the handicrafts declined school training took the place of the old shop training. Art instruction was introduced in the public schools and art schools were organized on every hand. But while the art school training was broader than the shop training, it was not as thorough within its field. The old shop-trained carvers and coach and sign painters had a narrow knowledge, but they knew what they knew thoroughly. The same cannot be said for the school-trained artists of the nineteenth century.

The great period of American folk art covers about two hundred years, from the second quarter of the seventeenth century up to the third quarter of the nineteenth. During that time it was produced consistently and on a fairly large scale. The most productive sections were New England and Pennsylvania which were centers of craftsmanship in the colonial and early republican periods. The bulk of the objects in this exhibition were gathered in these localities. New York, New Jersey, and the states of the South and the Middle West have yielded a fair number of examples. There is another type of American folk art, found in the Southwestern states, particularly in New Mexico, which is not included in this exhibition. This art has a marked Spanish influence, is largely religious in character, and is related to Mexican colonial art. Spanish influence may also be discovered in the folk art of some of the Gulf States. On the Atlantic seaboard

8

the dominant influence is English, with German, Dutch, and French influences strong in certain regions, and a smattering of others, such as, for instance, that of the Far East. (See No. 77.)

The influence of the Far East came into such seaports as Salem, Newburyport, Boston, and New York with the ships that brought in cargoes from India, China, and Japan. The Chinese fad fostered in England in the eighteenth century by the work of Sir William Chambers and Thomas Chippendale had its reverbera-tions in America. It is true that the Chinese vogue consisted of rather poor imi-tations of porcelain, of decorated paper hangings, and an adaptation of Chinese furniture, but the influence was there nevertheless. Sea captains from the end of the eighteenth century brought in examples of Far Eastern art which found curi-ous reflections in American popular art. American trade with the Far East flourished in the early nineteenth century. By 1840 the China trade alone had reached the annual figure of seventy-five millions.

The European influence was brought in by the first colonists and it came into the seaports with almost every ship. Many of the makers of American folk art had seen European paintings and sculptures, or copies of them made by artists who had been in Europe. Most of them had seen pictures of works of art in books. They borrowed freely, but borrowing has not been disdained by the greatest masters, in fact one of the signs of a vital art is the ability to assimilate the work of others. In New England newspapers of the early eighteenth century there are many advertisements offering prints, such as prospects of Boston and other cities, harbor views, maps, "effigies" of notable people, and copies of European works of art. John Smibert advertised in the *Boston News-Letter* in 1735 to sell a collection of prints "after the finest paintings in Italy, France, Holland, and England, done by Raphael, Michael Angelo, Poussin, Rubens, and others of the greatest Masters." Smibert and John Watson brought over from England copies of European paintings. American artists who could afford to make the European tour usually made copies of paintings by the masters with a view to selling them when they returned home. By the beginning of the nine-teenth century newspapers and magazines, through the publication of engrav-ings, stimulated a popular interest in art. Many magazines were founded in the first decade of the nineteenth century, and by the end of that decade there were twenty-seven or more daily newspapers in this country. There were also the lithographs of Currier & Ives and other print makers. Lithographs were pub-lished in America as early as 1819, and in the 1820's there were several firms of lithographers in New York, Boston, and Philadelphia. Nathaniel Currier was established in New York in the 1830's. The business of Currier & Ives lived out the century. They issued more than 4,000 titles and sold as many as 75,000 copies of their more popular prints. *Georgie—Quite Tired* (No. 32) was copied from a Currier & Ives print. It is well known that the makers of velvet and tinsel pictures got many of their patterns from the print makers.

The greatest production in American folk art was in painting. Under the head of painting come inn signs, shop signs, limner portraits, landscapes, sailing pictures, a great variety of decorative paintings, and paintings on velvet and glass. The sculpture is of many varieties—decorative and architectural carvings, ships' figureheads, weather-vanes, shop signs and trade symbols like the cigar store Indians, gravestones, lawn figures, hitching posts, fire insurance emblems, plates of heat-holding stoves decorated in relief, doorstops, toys, and a host of miscellaneous objects.

Folk art was called out by various demands. Limner portraits were in great demand before the days of photography. Itinerant makers of "counterfeit presentments" were a standard feature of American life from the late seventeenth century to the middle of the nineteenth. Before the advance of popular education in the first half of the nineteenth century taverns and shops needed carved and painted signs to attract attention. These may be considered the ancestors of the present-day billboards and electric signs. Today only the barber, the jeweller, and the pawnbroker keep consistently to the old style, but in the days when the mass of the people could not read and when buildings had no numbers, shopkeepers, innkeepers, artisans, and even some of the professions advertised themselves by means of symbolical signs. There was the sheaf of wheat in front of the bakeshop, a boot advertised the bootmaker, a hand the glovemaker, a tooth the dentist, and so on.

Figureheads were always in demand at seaports up to the end of the clipper ship era shortly after the Civil War. The demand for weather-vanes and wild fowl decoys has continued to the present day. Besides these kinds of folk art, usually made by craftsmen, there has always been the amateur type. Some of the most beautiful pieces of amateur folk art were made by women. These are the still lifes, flower pieces, and mourning pictures painted on velvet, and delicate watercolors of birds, flowers, fruit and foliage. Women in colonial and early American days, before they were drawn into the factory system, were skilled in the handicrafts. They knew how to sew, spin, weave, embroider, how to dye fabrics, and how to make the dyes which they used. Their knowledge of textiles and of dyes explains the quality of the velvet paintings which they made. (See Nos. 79 to 111.)

Most of these velvet paintings, which are a distinct contribution to the tradition of still-life painting in this country, were made between 1800 and 1840 by young women in the seminaries and academies which sprang up all over the United States after the Revolution. These schools, intended for the children of the middle stratum of American society, taught the three R's, natural history, and moral philosophy, and among the "extras" were such appealing arts as fancy work, plain sewing, drawing, watercolor painting, painting on glass and velvet, and waxwork. The students were taught to copy prints, paint flowers and foliage after patterns, and to paint imaginative pictures which were called "fancy pieces." In the early nineteenth century, when the art of embroidery had temporarily declined, it was considered necessary for every genteel young lady to be able to paint, and painting on velvet was very popular.

The subjects of the velvet paintings were usually arrangements of fruit and flowers, or more rarely, landscapes and figures. There is a family resemblance in the designs of these paintings, most of which were made after patterns or traditional motifs, but there is a good deal of originality in the treatment of the oft-repeated theme, especially in the use of color, and the artists must be credited with good taste in selecting designs. Velvet paintings were sometimes drawn directly on the material, or the outlines were marked by sifting powder through the holes in pricked paper patterns. More often the designs were applied to the fabric by means of a set of stencils known as "theorems." The making of these theorems was an elaborate bit of work, which the young lady students could avoid by purchasing theorems ready made from professional artists, or by using patterns supplied by the schools. The catalogue of the Literary and Scientific Institution at Brandon, Vt., where Susan Whitcomb, painter of *The Residence of Gen. Washington* (No. 56), studied in the 1840's, lists an "extra for drawing or painting with use of patterns, $1.00." Velvets have been called theorem paintings, but not all of them were made with theorems, and theorems were used for other kinds of paintings as well. A nineteenth century writer says: "This style of painting is done under several names, viz., Theorem Painting, Poonah Painting, Oriental Painting, Formula Painting, Stencilling, etc. It is better adapted to fruit, birds, and butterflies than to landscapes and heads. It will enable you to paint on paper, silk, velvet, crape, and light-colored wood."

The most extensive field of American folk art is that of portraiture. There seems always to have been a good market for portraits in this country. It is natural that portraits should be more popular than other types of painting because in addition to their esthetic value, they appeal to family pride and the desire for social prestige. A few of the stricter Puritans and Quakers looked upon painting as a manifestation of worldly pride and extravagance, but there were as many people in the greatest age of Greece who denounced the arts as there were among the people of early New England. The statements of a few rock-ribbed individuals have been expanded into a creed for the whole population of colonial America. The Puritans, and not a few of the Quakers, with all their dislike of the vanities of this world, did not hesitate to patronize the portrait painter.

Before the days of the daguerreotype the limner had an important place in the community. He was one of the permanent features of New England village life, and there were many itinerants who traveled from one plantation to another in the South, though it has been stated that the wealthy Southerners preferred to have portraits painted in London, even if they had to have them painted after a written description. The South had a number of able painters early in the seventeenth century. Henrietta Johnson, who died in Charleston, S. C., in 1728, and who has become known as the first woman painter in America, made a number of pastel portraits of the limner type. B. Roberts advertised in the *South Carolina Gazette* in 1735 that he was prepared to do "Portrait painting, Engraving, Heraldry, and House painting." Henry Warren advertised in Williamsburg, Va., in 1768 that he would paint "family pieces." The itinerant limners were usually carriage, house, and sign painters, though professional painters like Gustavus Hesselius, Charles Bridges, John Smibert, and others traveled about the country. Many of the best American painters have not been averse to painting signs, among them Gilbert Stuart, Benjamin West, Francis Alexander, Charles Willson Peale, Thomas Moran, Alexander H. Wyant, and in our own time, "Pop" Hart.

The portrait painters knew how to turn their hands to many tasks. They painted signs, coats-of-arms, coaches, and houses, and there seems little doubt that it is to them that we must ascribe the wall paintings in colonial houses in New England, New York, and the South, and possibly also the painting of floors with the stencil designs which may be observed in a number of portraits in this exhibition. (See *The Blue Boy*, No. 3, *The Girl in White*, No. 4, and *Helen Eddy*, No. 5.) Some of these wall and floor paintings were done by European artists who came to this country (like the Neapolitan, Michel Felice Corné, who lived in America from 1792 to 1845), but most of them appear to be work of native craftsmen. There was a good deal of decorative painting for these men to do in colonial and early American days, the painting of furniture, chests, trays, clock-faces, mirror tops, bandboxes, bride boxes, etc.

Most of the old portrait painters are nameless, though here and there one of them comes out of the shadows of anonymity. The well-known Chester Harding was a backwoods chair maker, innkeeper, and sign painter before he became a portrait painter. The first paintings he saw were the work of an itinerant limner. He was so excited by them that he sat down at once to imitate them by painting a portrait of his wife. His career as a painter began with that picture and soon he was traveling about New England and the western territories painting farmers and merchants at forty dollars a head. His accomplishments amazed the aged Daniel Boone, of whom he painted a portrait, and they won him favor with the elite of Boston, and with the British nobility.

The portrait-painting itinerants were the forerunners of American quantity production methods. In winter, when travel was difficult, they made sets of stock pictures, painting in the background, clothing, accessories, and hands. These pictures were usually in pairs, male and female. The clothing in the limner stock pictures was in line with the fashions of the period, with men's coats and waistcoats of a solid and conventional cut, and for the women dresses of rich stuffs decked with lace and ribbons. The backgrounds were usually arranged with pillars and decorative hangings, though some limners, like the painter of *The Blue Boy* and *The Girl in White* favored cloud halos and painted floors. The accessories were of various kinds, well-bound books with Latin and French titles, newspapers, prayer-books, spectacles, and bouquets of flowers. With these accessories the painter usually tried to suggest the vocation of the sitter, using telescopes for sea captains, law books for lawyers, medical books for physicians, etc.

In the springtime the limner would set out with his lot of headless portraits and go from town to town hunting heads. The stock figure was one of the limner's best sales arguments, for what housewife could resist the fine dresses, the meticulously painted lace, and the lovely hands which the painter had prepared for her? This method of painting also had considerable influence upon the limner himself, for in preparing the stock figure in the absence of the sitter he became interested primarily in design. Even where the design is not distin-

13

guished the picture is usually held together by a telling pattern of light and dark. Usually there was something which the limner could do well; he might be good at getting a likeness, or at suggesting the texture of garments. Most of the old limners seem to have taken a delight in the treatment of textile surfaces, especially when they were painting the details of women's costumes. The painters' method of working and their limited training made for a certain monotony, and for a tendency to use formulae in the painting of stock figures. They were apt to insist too much upon outline, and upon detail which was not essential. The flat treatment of the clothing and accessories in the stock figures sometimes made it difficult for the painter to combine the more realistic modeling of the face with the flat color and summary handling of planes in the prepared figure. This difficulty often appears in the later portraits. In the earlier ones contours are handled with precision and the light and shade in the face is kept to a minimum, and this harmonizes very well with the treatment of the stock figures.

The fee for the limner portraits ranged from eight to forty dollars. The number of these portraits painted before the advent of photography must have been enormous. A great number of them have found their way to the junk heap, or have been destroyed in one way or another. Most of them were bad; but there is a fair number which is good, and a small number which is excellent. In the better portraits such as *Mr. Harrison* and *Mrs. Harrison* (Nos. 14 and 15), *Man with Jabot* (No. 16), and *Man with White Stock* (No. 38), it is remarkable how much of the individuality of the sitter the limner has been able to get into the picture. In the very best of them, such as *Portrait of a Man* (No. 34), *Woman Holding Book* (No. 35) and in the children's portraits (Nos. 3, 4, 5, 7, etc.) there is directness, unity, inventiveness, a veracious attempt to set down the character of the subject, and a personal quality which is not always to be found in the work of some of our acclaimed masters.

In American folk art landscapes and genre paintings are much rarer than portraits. There were not many landscapes painted in this country up to the close of the eighteenth century, and most of these were topographical pictures, harbor views, etc. Nathaniel Emmons who died in 1740 is said to have painted landscapes, but the only evidence for this is a newspaper notice at the time of his death which said that "Some of his Pieces are such admirable imitations of nature, both in faces, River Banks and Rural Scenes that the pleased Eye can not easily leave them." None of his landscapes is known to be in existence. Ralph

Earl is the greatest American landscape painter of the eighteenth century, but his masterpiece in this field, *Leicester Hills*, in the Worcester Museum, was painted in the first year of the nineteenth century. This picture has much in common with folk painting, and so, it appears from the engravings of them made by Amos Doolittle, had Earl's pictures of the battles of Concord and Lexington, the originals of which have disappeared. Smibert is said to have painted landscapes, Benjamin West at the beginning of his career painted one or two, but there was little demand for anything but portraits in America in the eighteenth century, and even in England such men as Gainsborough and Richard Wilson had no easy time finding purchasers for landscapes. American landscape did not really get under weigh until the nineteenth century.

The landscapes are not as standardized as the portraits. They have more originality and variety. Among the most original of the landscape painters were the anonymous makers of rather crude mural paintings on the walls of houses in Connecticut, Massachusetts, and Maine. Of the known men who painted landscape, genre, and historical and allegorical pictures three whose work has great originality and personal force are included in this exhibition. These are Edward Hicks and Joseph Pickett, both of Bucks County, and M. Boyle, of Carlisle, Pennsylvania, who painted *The Capture of Major André* (No. 20). Hicks was a pious Quaker sign painter whose avocation was making allegorical and historical landscapes which included *William Penn's Treaty with the Indians, The Grave of William Penn* (No. 22), and *The Peaceable Kingdom* (No. 21). Most of these were painted between 1830 and 1849, when business was slow in Hicks' shop. The most notable of them is *The Peaceable Kingdom*, of which Hicks painted several versions, no one of them exactly like the others. Hicks' painting of landscape in these pictures associates him with the forerunners of the Hudson River school. Both pictures have compositional qualities of a high order, the grouping in *The Grave of William Penn* is well handled and in *The Peaceable Kingdom* it is handled with mastery.

The work of Edward Hicks may be called naïve, but its naïveté is an expression of something which artists are always striving to retain, innocence of vision. Hicks had innocence of vision and simplicity and freshness of expression, and he had knowledge too. The knowledge was limited to what he had learned in the sign and carriage painting shop, but it was a clear and well-tried knowledge, solidly grounded in a craft tradition and not based on theory. In his mastery of this narrow range of knowledge, his innocence of vision, and the religious intensity which inspired his work Hicks is akin to the European primitives. Hicks may be called an American Rousseau who antedated the Douanier by half a century. He created a personal style which is unmistakable.

Another man whose style is unmistakable is Joseph Pickett, painter of *Manchester Valley* (No. 24). It appears that he was entirely self-taught, and that his work is the expression of sheer genius. The only craft he knew was that of carpentry, and from this he may have got the idea of good joinery and sound construction which his work shows so clearly. Pickett was a carpenter and storekeeper at New Hope, Pennsylvania. Late in life he was seized with the ambition to paint the history of his native town, and he knew so little about painting that he had to improvise his technique and even his tools as he went along. It is said that like Benjamin West he drew the hair of the domestic cat through goose quills to make brushes, and he eked out his restricted palette with the juice of berries, and with the red clay of the Delaware hills. Pickett drew like a child, and often built up his figures in relief, sometimes as high as half an inch above the canvas. He knew nothing of abstract devices to suggest space forward and back, and he naturally fell into the use of isometric perspective because he wanted to give equal importance to many objects in the picture. In the *Manchester Valley* he achieves a design of extraordinary quality through an inversion of perspective. For all his technical idiosyncrasies there is in his work a plastic sense, and a craftsmanship of a high order. His use of sand to suggest the texture of stone and his inversion of perspective relate his work directly to certain modern tendencies. His sense of movement, his space division, and his feeling for the right relation between areas of color place such a work as *Manchester Valley* among the masterpieces of American folk art.

The work of men like Hicks and Pickett bears the impress of strong personalities who adapted to their own ends the folk traditions from which their art springs. This is true also of M. Boyle, the painter of *The Capture of Major André* (No. 20), of Joseph Stock, painter of *Helen Eddy* (No. 5), and of the anonymous painters of *Child with Dog* (No. 2), *Baby in Red High Chair* (No. 1), and *Child in Blue Dress* (No. 7). Even when these folk artists were influenced to the point of directly imitating the work of others, they translated what they imitated with a strong personal idiom. Artists like these usually worked in localities remote from the centers of population, where they had little material for study and had to rely on the methods of their craft, or on their own imagination, inventing their technique and symbols as they went along. Since the folk art tradition is a tradition of craftsmanship which comes out of the handling of tools and materials, it is natural that the influence of specific crafts should be strong. Carriage and sign painters stuck to the flat colors and the precision of outline which is characteristic of their trade. Even when they tried their hand at modeling in painting faces, they stuck to the sign-painter style in the painting of clothing and background.

The quality of American folk art which first strikes the observer is quaintness, and this is particularly true of the folk art which comes out of Pennsylvania. Very quaint are the decorative pictures celebrating birth and baptism which are to be found in all the counties of Pennsylvania settled by the Germans. These are the "fracturs" (Nos. 72 to 78), which come out of a distinct local tradition in American folk painting, related directly to medieval manuscript illumination. This art was brought to America by various German pietist orders, especially by the brethren who under the leadership of the strange visionary, Conrad Beissel, founded a religious community at Ephrata, in Lancaster County, in 1728. Fractur painting was practised extensively by the Pennsylvania Germans, and it was imitated to a certain extent by the English settlers. It is one of the instances of an art which flourished in America long after it was dead in Europe. The fracturs (the word is probably derived from the name of the old German gothic type) were usually drawn with a goose quill, and the colors laid in with cat's hair brushes. Henry Chapman Mercer, the founder of the Doylestown Museum, some years ago discovered a fractur-maker's paint box, a wooden box twelve inches long and six inches wide, with several compartments. The largest compartment contained "goose-quill pens and brushes made of the hair of the domestic cat." The smaller compartments held small bottles of "home-mixed inks and paints . . . , once liquefied in whiskey, and the varnish was composed of the gum of the cherry tree diluted in water."

Fractur, like Chinese painting, is closely related to calligraphy. There is almost no modeling. The third dimension is suggested by the use of line, but this is never carried very far. The color is gay, with red, green, yellow, and blue used with the greatest boldness. Fracturs are both religious and secular in subject, and it is in this field that one comes across most of the rather rare religious art of this country—if the New England gravestones are excepted. An example of the religious type of fractur is the *Crucifixion* (No. 73). There are also semi-religious, and secular pieces such as birth certificates (Nos. 74 and 75), wedding certificates, rewards of merit, bookmarks, portraits, landscapes, and drawings of birds and animals (*Bright Birds*, No. 78, and *The Peaceable Kingdom*, No. 76).

The secular fracturs were made by schoolmasters and their pupils. It appears that fractur was one of the standard courses in the curriculum of Pennsylvania German schools up to the middle of the nineteenth century. With the sole exception of the best missal illumination made by the brethren at Ephrata, whose work has a certain refinement and distinction, it is in this secular work that the masterpieces of fractur are to be found. Teaching of fractur in the Pennsylvania German schools appears to have been abandoned about the time of the Civil War, and when Henry Chapman Mercer discovered his fractur-maker's kit, the art had long been forgotten. Many of the fracturs are beautiful bits of decorative painting. The drawing has a lovely linear rhythm, and the color is good. One of the masterpieces of the fractur art is the magnificent *Horse with Saddle* (No. 72), found in Bucks County, Pennsylvania.

Birth and death inspired the fractur maker beyond any other subjects. Death as a subject is pervasive in American folk art. It has been treated by a great many carvers and painters. The New England gravestone carvers treated it with medieval imagination. A more sentimental treatment of it is found in the mourning pictures showing willow trees and drooping figures of relatives about the tomb. The most interesting examples are those painted on velvet (Nos. 106 and 107), presumably by the young ladies in boarding school who made most of the velvet paintings, which are to be found in every section of the Atlantic seaboard.

It is not unusual in American folk art to find the influence of one technique upon another. In the early nineteenth century work various techniques were mingled. Drawing, painting and embroidery were not infrequently used together in the same pictures, the drawing and painting handled in such a way as to imitate the effect of embroidery. An effect of the embroidery technique may be observed in Susan Whitcomb's watercolor of Mt. Vernon (No. 56), the watercolor *Rebecca at the Well* (No. 48), and the velvet painting *Ruth and Naomi* (No. 108). Velvet technique is evident in many of the watercolors and pastels, and this no doubt has some relation to the use of the same stencils for painting in different media. (See Design Group, Nos. 118–122.) The design and to a certain extent the technique in the watercolors *Basket of Fruit* (No. 63) and *Still Life with Watermelons* (No. 64) are similar to those in the velvet painting *Still Life with Watermelons* (No. 81), and suggest that the same "theorems" may have been used. In the pastel *Mountain Landscape* (No. 37) the velvet technique achieves a very beautiful result. The technique of the painter of *The True Cross* (No. 23) was probably based on memories of tapestries which he had seen. In the *Glass Bowl with Fruit* (No. 62) there is just a hint of the technique of the tinsel picture, though it appears certain that no theorems could have been used in the painting of a picture of this type. The *Glass Bowl with Fruit*, in its sensitive drawing, its delicacy of modeling, and beautiful clarity of design, is one of the most masterly American watercolors of the early nineteenth century.

Portraits, still lifes, and landscapes painted on glass were popular in England in the latter half of the eighteenth century, and this popularity was reflected in the colonies. Most of the glass pictures were made after engravings (No. 115), or by attaching an engraving to the back of the glass with varnish, then removing the paper of the engraving and applying color to the design which remained (No. 116). From the early part of the eighteenth century there were many notices in New England papers advertising "metsotintos for painting on glass." The art of glass painting was practised to a considerable extent by the New Englanders and the Pennsylvania Germans. The glass paintings in this collection date from the nineteenth century. Numbers 112 and 114 were made in Pennsylvania, numbers 113 and 117 in New England. Glass painting in New England was more apt to be of a kind which combined the use of colored tinsel laid on the back of glass with oil paint. Some very striking still lifes of fruits and of flowers were achieved in this medium (*Urn of Roses with Butterflies*, No. 117).

There is even greater variety in the field of folk sculpture than in that of painting. The earliest pieces of American sculpture were ships' figureheads, gravestone carvings, and weather-vanes. Ship building developed early in New England and the shipyards produced many good carvers. There was a ship-builder in Plymouth as early as 1623. Ships had to have figureheads, head rails, and stern boards, which were carved and painted, and they often had friezes on the various deck levels carved and painted, as well as the decorations in the cabins. One Captain Hawkins in 1645 "built a stately ship at Boston of 400 ton and upward and set her out with great ornament of carving and painting. . . ." All this work had to be accurately proportioned and fitted. It was a fine school for carvers and such men as Samuel McIntire, the wood-carver of Salem, and William Rush, who has been called the first American sculptor, came out of it. Like McIntire, many of the domestic architects of New England were carpenters and carvers who had been trained in the shipyards. Most of the earliest carvers had learned their trade in England or had it from men who were trained in the English shipyards, but the American work has a distinct quality. It is apt to have more crudeness and strength than one finds in the English work, greater simplicity in design and more restraint in ornamentation.

Very few of the early figureheads have survived because of the perishable nature of the material of which they were made and because of their exposure in all weathers. Most of the American figureheads now preserved date from the 'forties, 'fifties, and 'sixties of the last century, the period of clipper ships. The Boston Marine Museum has a figurehead by a local carver, Isaac Fowle, but the work of other carvers of Boston, such as the Skillings and Joseph Doherty, has passed into oblivion or into little-known private collections. There is a figurehead by William L. Seavey of Bangor, Maine, in the collection of the local Historical Society; a figurehead by Charles Sampson, one of the many carvers of Bath, Maine, is at Webb's Seamen's Home in New York City; a figurehead attributed to Samuel McIntire, the wood-carver of Salem, is in the Peabody Museum in that city. Not a single example of the figurehead carving of William Rush of Philadelphia is known to exist, though there is one attributed to him in the collection of the Reading Historical Society at Reading, Pennsylvania; nor is there any known example of the figureheads by John Bellamy of Portsmouth, though many of his decorative carvings are in various collections throughout the country. The work of Joseph True of Salem, who is supposed to have inspired Nathaniel Hawthorne to write *Drowne's Wooden Image*, also has disappeared.

Another ship-carver whose work has disappeared is Joseph Wilson of Newburyport, who carved a yard full of figures for one of the most celebrated of American eccentrics, "Lord" Timothy Dexter. Dexter was an illiterate but shrewd and venturesome Yankee trader who made a good deal of money in various odd enterprises. In keeping with what he conceived to be his station in life he took the title of "Lord," had his own poet laureate, and hired Wilson (and possibly others) to carve figures which he placed on pillars and arches about his estate in Newburyport. His first order to Wilson was for portraits of the three Presidents, Washington, Adams and Jefferson, and of Benjamin Franklin, John Hancock, Alexander Hamilton, "and Rouffous King and John Jea, and 2 granedears on the top of the hous, 4 Lions below, 1 Eagle, is on the Coupolow, . . . One Younecorne, one Dogg, Addam and Eave in the garden,—one horse. The houll (whole) is not concluded on as yet." All physical trace of Dexter, his estate, his statues, his commercial enterprises, has disappeared. All that is left is

his legend, and his book, *A Pickel for the Knowing Ones*, which in idea, or-
thography, and punctuation is certainly one of the most astonishing books ever
printed.

Here and there along the coast of New England, and sometimes in New York
and other seaport towns, figureheads which show some of the old carvers' art
show up from time to time. *Minnehaha* (No. 123) was discovered in the West
Indies by the late Max Williams. It is an exceptionally fine example of the
American carvers' art in its sweep of line, and in the elevation and expansion of
form which is the mark of good sculpture. It is probably a late eighteenth century piece. The *Bust of Girl* (No. 124) which was discovered at Bridgeport,
Connecticut, came from a schooner which sailed on Long Island Sound. It is a
nineteenth century carving. Its simplicity of treatment gives it an almost classic
quality, and its Victorian refinement suggests that it may have been copied from
one of the popular prints of the time. A few of the old figureheads are preserved
in collections throughout the country. The Sewalls of Bath, Maine, descendants
of a family of ship-builders, own several figureheads by anonymous carvers;
George Harding of Chicago has a fine collection; and there are several in the Museum of the City of New York, the New Bedford Whaling Museum, the Buffalo
Historical Society, and the American Folk Art Gallery in New York.

Cigar store Indians are related to the figureheads so far as the carving is concerned, but actually they belong to the tradition of trade signs. The first cigar
store figures appeared upon the scene in the time of Queen Anne, but they were
not limited to Indians—Sir Walter Raleighs, Highlanders, Punches, etc., were
popular. These figures were sometimes designed by the carver, but more often
they were adapted from contemporary illustrations and prints. They have remarkable variety, and it is seldom that two of them are alike. The greatest
vogue for cigar store Indians in this country was between 1850 and 1880. They
began to disappear in the 'nineties, and by the second decade of the twentieth
century most of them had passed into oblivion. A few of them have lingered on
into our time. Curiously enough the oldest known American cigar store figure is
still in existence and in the shop in Lancaster, Pennsylvania, in which it was first
displayed. It dates from 1770 and is a one-third life-size figure of a gentleman in
the costume of the late eighteenth century.

The earliest American cigar store Indians were probably made by carvers em-
ployed in shipyards. The best of them have a crude sturdiness, a boldness and
simplicity in the carving, and a distribution of color which gives them interest as

polychrome sculpture. The *Indian* (No. 125), with its compactness and primitive intensity, is a close relative of the figureheads. The *Trapper Indian* (No. 126) has a kind of baroque richness and dash. In the latter half of the nineteenth century, when the art of the figurehead carver had declined, the making of cigar store figures was taken up by Swiss and Germans. Julius Theodore Melchers, the father of the painter, Gari Melchers, was a well-known carver of Indians in Detroit.

The methods of the late nineteenth century carvers of cigar store Indians are described by F. W. Weitenkampf writing in *The New York Times* for Aug. 3, 1890: "The wood used is generally white pine, which is bought in logs of various lengths at the spar yards. The artist begins by making the roughest kind of an outline—a mere suggestion of what the proportions of the figure are to be. In this he is guided by paper patterns. The log is blocked out with the axe into appropriate spaces for the head, the body down to the waist, the portion from there to the knee, the rest of the legs (which are at once divided), and the feet . . . The feeling for form in the chopped block is so very elementary as to have complete suggestiveness only for the practiced artist. A hole is now bored in each end of the prepared log about 5 inches deep. Into each hole an iron bolt is placed, the projecting parts of which rest on supports so that the body hangs free. The carver now goes from the general to the particular. The surface of the wood soon becomes chipped up by the chisel and the log generally takes on more definite form. . . . Then when the figure is completely evolved the finishing touches are put in with finer tools. Detached hands and arms are made separately and joined to the body with screws. Then the various portions are appropriately painted, the whole is set on a stand running on wheels, and it is ready for delivery."

Weather-vanes are closely related to the figureheads because patterns from which many of them were cast and stamped were made by the same men who carved the figureheads and the shop signs. These weather-vanes are usually not as fine, sculpturally, as the figureheads, but there are more of them. Thousands of barns in New England and all through the states of the Atlantic seaboard have weather-vanes decorated with figures of men and animals. There are Indians, horses, cows, whales, roosters, pigeons, eagles, etc., carved in wood, or cut out, stamped, and cast in iron, copper, tin, lead, and other metals. Occasionally one comes across an indubitable masterpiece, such as the *Formal Horse* (No. 149). The *Horse with Flowing Tail* (No. 150) is one of the most decorative of the metal vanes. Currier & Ives prints of well-known race horses were much used by the makers of weather-vanes. *Horse and Sulky* (No. 151) is no doubt made after a print of one of the favorites of the turf.

The weather-vane makers were keen observers of animals, and many of them knew a good deal about design. There is a remarkable contrast between the tenseness and spirit of the horses and the *Cow* (No. 157) with its sensitively modeled body, thin at the neck, soft and full at the sides, the calm of the pose enhanced by flattened curves. In the *Formal Rooster* (No. 153) there is keen observation and a masterly handling of the decorative elements of design. The *Stylized Rooster* (No. 136) is a good piece of decorative carving in which the contrast between the soft down of the head and breast and the heavier feathers of the wings and tail is brought out by simple but effective conventions. The Pennsylvania Dutch were very successful in carving roosters which they painted with their characteristic colors. *Rooster* (No. 137), is typical. Another Pennsylvania vane is *Pheasant* (No. 155), a beautifully drawn silhouette cut out of iron.

The eagle has always been a popular subject in American folk art. When Washington made his first triumphal tour of the republic after his election it is said that he was greeted everywhere with displays of painted and carved images of the eagle, which had just been adopted as the national emblem. Since that time the wood-carvers have made thousands of eagles, and among these thousands there appears, now and then, a masterpiece. The *Eagle* (No. 132) is one of these. The majestic balance and energy of the pose, the continuous flow of contours, the variety and sensitiveness of the surface treatment make it the most remarkable piece of its kind discovered in this country. A fine example of decorative carving, probably intended as an ornament over the doorway of a ship's cabin, is the *Eagle* (No. 131) which is reproduced on the cover of this catalogue.

In number and variety wild fowl decoys lead the field in American folk sculpture. Decoys were made for purely utilitarian purposes, and are particularly interesting as the sculptural expression of the common man. Professional decoy makers, blacksmiths, carpenters, hunters, and whittlers in every section of the country where there is bird hunting turn them out in great numbers every year. They are a form of folk expression which has survived the machine age, for though many of them are made in factories, most of them are whittled by hand. Those made in factories are usually realistic, but the best of the hand-whittled decoys are not so much representations as abstract symbols. Each section of the country has its characteristic style. Fine specimens have been discovered in the Barnegat Bay section of New Jersey, around the Great South Bay on Long Island, on the New England coast, along the Mississippi, and in the South. The Doylestown, Pennsylvania, Museum has a number of decoys and there are a number in private collections, the most notable of which is that of Joel D. Barber, the architect. A number of sculptors and painters have also made collections of decoys. The two loon decoys (Nos. 145 and 146) have a decorative quality which indicates that they may have been made for ornamental purposes rather than for hunting. The miniature ducks (No. 147) from Barnegat Bay may possibly have been used as window signs by a decoy maker.

Most American folk sculptures were made for use, with decoration as a secondary object. Occasionally, however, one finds things which have no apparent basis in utility but which were made simply for the pleasure of the making. One of the most interesting fields for the collector of folk art is that of the whittler pieces made by carpenters, sailors, farmers, and others. The most remarkable piece of this type included in this exhibition is the *Henry Ward Beecher* (No. 127), which was carved by an Indiana farmer. In its simplicity of convention, and its combination of crude power, intimacy, and intensity, this piece is one of the most striking examples of American folk sculpture. Another fine piece is the *Seated Woman* (No. 129), made by an anonymous Pennsylvania German carver. There is a certain monumentality, a feeling of bulk in the square masses of the figure. The stylization of the wavy hair and the handling of the carved and painted diagonals of the dress trimming are extremely decorative.

Toys, such as the *Primitive Horse* (No. 139), the polychromed *Rooster* (No. 130), and the *Eagle* (No. 134), were probably made by country whittlers. Toys are an extensive field for the amateur of folk art. The counties of Pennsylvania settled by the Germans are filled with toys attributed to an ubiquitous carver called Schimmel. Schimmel's date is uncertain. Some say that he was a veteran of the Mexican War, others that he fought in the Civil War and was wounded at the battle of Gettysburg. It is supposed that he wandered about Pennsylvania, mainly in the Cumberland Valley, carving toys for farmers' children. The *Eagle* (No. 134), which has the crude power of peasant art, is attributed to him. There are too many of the so-called "Schimmel toys" to be the work of one man. Possibly there was a Schimmel, but his style of carving, which is very close to German peasant art, has evidently been imitated by others. The most beautiful of the toys carved in Pennsylvania is the type known as "Pennsylvania pine," of

24

which number 130 is one of the finest examples. Numbers 140, 141, 142, 143, and 144 are toys.

A type of folk sculpture local to the communities settled by Germans in Pennsylvania and the South are the plates of the so-called jamb stove. Five of these iron plates fastened together made a heat-holding stove which was built into the back of a fireplace. Hot embers were shoveled into these stoves and they warmed the room on the opposite side of the fireplace. Benjamin Franklin in a pamphlet written in 1744 described them as follows: "The German stove is like a Box, one side wanting. 'Tis composed of five iron plates scru'd together and fixed so that you may put Fuel into it from another room, or from Outside of the House. 'Tis a kind of oven reversed, its Mouth being without, and Body within the Room that is to be warmed by it."

The two side plates and the end plate of these stoves were decorated in relief. The designs for these stove plates were carved in wood. In the best of the plates the drawing is bold and incisive, the design is simple and well controlled, and there is a good deal of quaintness and humor in the treatment of the subjects. The most interesting plates are those decorated with biblical subjects, such as the slaying of Abel, the temptation of Joseph, and the marriage at Cana, though many fine plates have decorative arrangements of the tulips and birds which are common in Pennsylvania German work. *The Peaceable Kingdom* (No. 160) was one of the favorite biblical subjects, and *The Swarm of Bees* (No. 159), a favorite humorous subject. Both of them date from the middle of the eighteenth century.

Like so much in Pennsylvania German folk art, the stove plates are related to the peasant arts of Germany, and it is supposed that most of the carved patterns for the early plates were made by craftsmen who had been trained in Germany. Most of the plates were cast between 1735 and 1790, but the best period was between 1740 and 1760. Some of the best plates were made at Durham Furnace in Bucks County, at Warwick Furnace in Chester County, and also at Marlboro Furnace in the Shenandoah Valley. Number 159 was probably cast at Marlboro Furnace. Number 160 appears to have been cast in Pennsylvania, though it too may have come from Marlboro Furnace. These plates are not easy to find at this date. The late Henry Chapman Mercer gathered all the examples he could find in Pennsylvania and made the most complete collection of them now in existence.

In the first half of the nineteenth century ceramic "cottage ornaments" were fashionable in England and in America. Less known than these cottage ornaments are the plaster or chalkware figurines made mostly by the Pennsylvania

Germans. These chalkware pieces (see Nos. 163–175) were often made in imitation of Staffordshire figures, and while they are cruder than the figures which they imitated, they are often better in design and color and are among the most interesting examples of American polychromed small sculpture. Most of the chalkware figures now in existence were made after 1850, though the *Bust of a Man* (No. 163) appears to be earlier. The art of making these plasterware figures was known in this country in the eighteenth century. As early as 1768 Henry Christian Geyer advertised the making of plaster animals, and two years later his advertisement in the *Boston News-letter* of January 25 read: "Henry Christian Geyer, Stone Cutter, near Liberty Tree, South End, Boston, Hereby informs his Customers, and other Gentlemen and Ladies, that besides carrying on the Stone Cutting Business as usual, he carries on the Art and Manufacture of a Fuser Simulacrorum, or the making of all sorts of Images, viz., 1st. Kings and Queens; 2nd. King George & Queen Charlotte; 3rd. King & Queen of Prussia; 4th. King & Queen of Denmark; 5th. King & Queen of Sweden, Likewise a Number of Busts, among which are, Mathew Prior, Homer, Milton, &c.—also a number of animals such as Parrots, Dogs, Lions, Sheep, with a number of others too many to enumerate:—Said Geyer also cleans old deficient Animals, and makes them look as well as new, at a reasonable Rate. All the above mentioned Images, Animals, &c. are made of Plaister of Paris of this Country Produce, and Manufactured at a reasonable Rate . . . any Merchants, Masters of Vessels, Country Traders, Shopkeepers, &c., may be supplied with what quantity they may have occasion for by giving timely notice to said Geyer."

The list of objects which come under the head of American folk art is practically inexhaustible. There are hitching posts with the heads of horses and eagles; bootjacks; doorstops; architectural ornaments; fire insurance emblems (No. 161) which used to be put on houses in the late eighteenth and early nineteenth century when putting out a fire was the business of the fire insurance companies; lawn figures like the *George Washington* (No. 148); and dogs and stags of lead and other metals that used to decorate lawns in Victorian days (many of these made in England). Several firms in New York made lawn figures and weather-vanes wholesale for the country trade. As Currier & Ives were the print makers to the American people so these firms were its sculptors.

Public interest in American folk art is a development of the past few years. The discoverers of its esthetic quality were the pioneers of modern art who began coming back to this country from France about 1910. These artists were in revolt against the naturalistic and impressionistic tendencies of the nineteenth century, and their emphasis upon a return to the sources of tradition had given them an interest in primitive and naïve art. They first turned to the productions of the American aborigines which they found in natural history museums. There were few pieces of American folk art in public collections at that time, and these were mostly in the museums of historical societies where they were valued for their relation to local history, or simply as curiosities. The cult of Americana had begun but it centered about the crafts of the silversmith, the potter, and the furniture maker, and, so far as the fine arts are concerned, in the work of painters like Copley and Stuart. About 1920, artists, rummaging through antique shops and farmers' attics for old American furniture came across pictures which arrested their attention. Most of these pictures were merely quaint, but some of them had esthetic value of a high order, and all of them had a quality which gave them a certain kinship with modern art.

The interest in American folk art spread from the artists to the collectors and museum directors. The first public exhibitions of American folk painting were those shown by Mrs. Juliana R. Force at the Whitney Studio Club, and by the Dudensing Gallery, in New York; by Mr. and Mrs. Elie Nadelman in their folk museum at Riverdale-on-Hudson, New York; and by Mrs. Isabel Carleton Wilde in her shop in Cambridge, Massachusetts. The first public exhibitions of American folk sculpture were those of Mr. and Mrs. Elie Nadelman in their museum at Riverdale-on-Hudson, and of the Newark Museum. All these exhibitions have been held within the past ten years. In the last year or two there have been exhibitions of American folk painting and sculpture shown by the Harvard Society for Contemporary Art in Cambridge, Massachusetts, the Newark Museum in Newark, New Jersey, the Whitney Museum of American Art in New York, the Detroit Society of Arts and Crafts, the Albright Gallery in Buffalo, and the American Folk Art Gallery and the Hackett Gallery in New York.

Any judgment upon American folk art at this time can represent little more than a personal opinion. The whole field still needs intensive research and study. Yet some tentative judgments may be ventured. Folk art cannot be valued as highly as the work of our greatest painters and sculptors, but it is certainly entitled to a place in the history of American art. When compared with the work of our secondary masters it holds its own very well. Few American paintings are

27

better works of art than *Manchester Valley* (No. 24), *The Peaceable Kingdom* (No. 21), *Child with Dog* (No. 2), *Mountain Landscape* (No. 37), *Glass Bowl with Fruit* (No. 62), and *Still Life* (No. 79). Few American sculptures are the peers of *Minnehaha* (No. 123), *Eagle* (No. 132), *Formal Horse* (No. 149), and *Formal Rooster* (No. 153). There is no doubt that these works have many technical deficiencies from the academic and naturalistic point of view, but with the artists who made them realism was a passion and not merely a technique. Surface realism meant nothing to them. It might be contended that this results from a lack of technical proficiency. The actual reason appears to be that the folk artists tried to set down not so much what they saw as what they knew and what they felt. Their art mirrors the sense and the sentiment of a community, and is an authentic expression of American experience.

HOLGER CAHILL

CATALOG

An asterisk before a catalog number indicates that the work is illustrated by a plate bearing the same number. Except where otherwise mentioned the artist's name is unknown.

OIL PAINTINGS

*1 BABY IN RED HIGH CHAIR, *about* 1790. *Oil on canvas.* H. 21½″ W. 14¾″
Pennsylvania German. Found in New York

*2 CHILD WITH DOG, *about* 1800. *Oil on canvas.* H. 23½″ W. 14½″
Found in Massachusetts

*3 THE BLUE BOY, *about* 1830. *Oil on canvas.* H. 42″ W. 28″
Found in Bridgeport, Connecticut. Brother of The Girl in White

*4 THE GIRL IN WHITE, *about* 1830. *Oil on canvas.* H. 34¼″ W. 24¾″
Found in Bridgeport, Connecticut. Sister of The Blue Boy

*5 HELEN EDDY, *about* 1840. *Oil on canvas.* H. 40¼″ W. 28″
By Joseph Stock, 1815–1855

Joseph Stock was born and lived his forty years of life in Springfield, Massachusetts. He was a cripple, and had to get about in a wheelchair. It appears that he was self taught. Very little else is known about him. He advertised his work in the Springfield directory from 1846 to 1852. These advertisements indicate that daguerreotypes were in far greater demand than Stock's painted portraits, even at the low price of $8 a head. His advertisement of 1846 follows: "Stock and Cooley. Portrait and Daguerrean Gallery. Opposite Chicopee Bank, Main St. Where the public are respectfully invited to call and examine their specimens of painting and superb colored daguerreotype. Likenesses taken in a superior manner on large or small size plates, and in groups of from two to seven persons. A perfect and satisfactory likeness guaranteed. Likenesses taken of deceased persons. Instructions carefully given, and pupils furnished with everything necessary for the business at prices varying from $.75 to $1.50. Photographs put up in breast-pins, lockets, cases, frames from $2 upwards. Portraits, from $8 to $25. To daguerreotype operators—German cameras, lockets, plates, cases, chemicals, polishing materials and all articles used in the business furnished to order." Stock's partnership with Cooley evidently did not last long, for the next directory records Stock as located at East State Street, Springfield, where he painted portraits and miniatures over Stocking & Cate's grocery store. By 1849 we find him located in the Foot block, and though not working with his former partner his advertisement comes at the close of Cooley's:

"Mr. Stock has rooms directly over the gallery and is prepared to execute orders for portrait, landscape, banners and warranted satisfactory in every respect. Those having daguerreotypes of deceased friends can have them copied in size of life and a faithful likeness of the original warranted. Specimens to be seen at the gallery." The last directory to list Mr. Stock was that of 1852. Ten paintings by Stock have been discovered. Most of these are full-length portraits. A number of his portraits are owned by his relatives. No example of the landscapes or banners of the advertisement have come to light

*6 CHILD WITH WOODPECKER, *about* 1840. *Oil on canvas.* H. 29½" W. 26"
Pennsylvania German. Found in New York

7 CHILD IN BLUE DRESS, *about* 1840. *Oil on canvas.* H. 26" W. 22"
Found in Maine

8 CHILD IN ROSE-COLORED DRESS, *about* 1840. *Oil on canvas.* H. 26½" W. 22½"
Found in Baltimore, Maryland

9 CHILD WITH WHIP, *late* 1820's. *Oil on wood.* H. 20¼" W. 16¼"
Found in Bridgeport, Connecticut

*10 THREE CHILDREN, *about* 1830. *Oil on wood.* H. 37" W. 37"
Found in Syracuse, New York

*11 GIRL ON BALCONY, 1840–1850. *Oil on canvas.* H. 38" W. 29¾"
Probably Pennsylvania German. Found at Bethlehem, Pennsylvania. May have come originally from the Shenandoah Valley

*12 BABY WITH DOLL, 1840–1850. *Oil on canvas.* H. 15½" W. 11¾"
Type of portrait found near Fall River, Massachusetts

13 GIRL WITH BASKET OF FLOWERS, *about* 1850. *Oil on canvas.* H. 24¾" W. 17¾"
Found in Reading, Pennsylvania

*14 MR. HARRISON, *about* 1815. *Oil on wood.* H. 33¾" W. 25½"
Found in New York. Uniform of the War of 1812. This and No. 15 are a pair

*15 MRS. HARRISON, *about* 1815. *Oil on wood.* H. 33¾" W. 25½"
Found in New York

16 MAN WITH JABOT, 1810–1820. *Oil on wood.* H. 26½″ W. 21¾″
Found in Bridgeport, Connecticut. This and No. 17 are a pair

17 WOMAN WITH LACE CAP AND RUFF, 1810–1820. *Oil on wood.* H. 26½″ W. 21¾″
Found in Bridgeport, Connecticut

*18 WASHINGTON AND LAFAYETTE AT THE BATTLE OF THE BRANDYWINE.
Late eighteenth century. *Oil on canvas.* H. 21″ W. 31¼″
Found in New York. Said to have come from an old tavern at Harvard, Massachusetts

*19 POCAHONTAS SAVING CAPTAIN JOHN SMITH, *date undetermined.* *Oil on canvas.* H. 29½″ W. 34¾″
Found in Baltimore, Maryland. This was a popular subject and was used by American print makers of the nineteenth century. This painting appears to antedate the known prints

*20 THE CAPTURE OF MAJOR ANDRÉ, *exact date undetermined.* *Oil on canvas.*
H. 27½″ W. 34¼″
By M. Boyle, Carlisle (signed).   Found in Carlisle, Pennsylvania.   Nothing is known about this artist, but one other painting by him, a still life, has been found

*21 THE PEACEABLE KINGDOM, *about* 1833. *Oil on canvas.* H. 17¼″ W. 23½″
By Edward Hicks, 1780–1849. "An illustration of the eleventh chapter of Isaiah and embracing all the animals therein mentioned in the foreground and in the distance William Penn treating with the Indians."

Edward Hicks was a Quaker preacher who made his living as a coach maker and painter, and as a house and sign painter. He painted signs for inns, shops, roads and bridges, made fire screens, and is said to have done portraits. When he was not busy preaching or working at his trade, he painted allegorical and historical pictures, "The Peaceable Kingdom," "Penn's Treaty with the Indians," "The Grave of William Penn," and others, making several versions of each subject.

Hicks was a deeply religious man. He preached at Quaker meetings in Pennsylvania, Maryland, New York, Ohio, Indiana and Canada. In 1825, with his cousin Elias Hicks of Jericho, Long Island, founder of the Hicksite sect of Quakers, he preached at Quaker meeting-houses in Rose and Hester Streets in New York. These sermons were published under the title of "Sermons Delivered by Elias Hicks and Edward Hicks in Friends' Meetings, New York, in the 5th Month, 1825." A book of his memoirs was published in Philadelphia in 1851. He also published a number of pamphlets of religious discourses, among them "A Little Present for Friends and Friendly People in the Form of a Miscellaneous Discourse by a Poor Illiterate Mechanic," and "A Work of Exhortation to Young Friends. Presented to Them Without

Money and Without Price. By a Poor Illiterate Minister." His memoirs are filled with religious exhortations and the most truly pious sentiment. His work as a painter is rarely mentioned.

Hicks was born at Attleborough, Bucks County, Pennsylvania, April 4, 1780. He was a descendant of Robert Hicks who landed at Plymouth in 1621 on the ship "Fortune," which followed the "Mayflower." At the age of thirteen he was apprenticed to a coach maker named Tomlinson at Four-Lanes-End near Attleborough. He remained there for seven years learning the coach making trade, especially the painting. He came to the coach shop a very pious boy, but, he says, "the tenderness of my religious impressions too soon wore off, and instead of weeping and praying I soon got to laughing and swearing; and having what may truly be called a natural fund of nonsense I soon became a favorite with my shop mates." In the coach shop days he says he was in danger of liking the ways of this world too much, but at twenty-one he turned again to religion. It was said of him that he "was favored with a renewed visitation of Heavenly love; and yielding thereto he passed through the dispensation of condemnation, which he viewed as baptism unto repentance, by which his former pleasures were marred, and the friendship and glory of the world were stained in his view. . . . about the 30th year of his age he came into the ministry, deeply in the cross to his natural will, . . . covering the meetings with that solemnity which is precious and comforting to those present . . ."

For a time after his religious conversion Hicks quit painting for farming which he thought more compatible with the Christian life, but he could not make a go of farming and had to return to his old business. In 1811 he moved to Newtown where, he says, "comparatively speaking every tenth house was a tavern." Shortly after his arrival in Newtown he got an order to paint a sign for a hotel, showing the proprietor with his coach-and-four. He painted the man with his hat over one eye and looking decidedly tipsy. When the proprietor saw it he said, "That man on the box looks as if he were drunk." Hicks replied, "Thee is usually that way and I wanted it to look natural." After the proprietor promised to try not to be drunk while driving his coach, Hicks repainted the sign.

A Friends' meeting house was built at Newtown soon after Hicks' arrival there and he became its minister. "Being fruitful he grew in his gift and became an eminent minister of the Gospel; adorning the doctrine he preached by a life corresponding therewith." During his ministry he labored "with his hands for the support of his family, so that he could say with the apostle, 'these hands have ministered to my necessities and those that were with me'." He believed in being diligent in business. His diary records now and then: "busy in my shop," "industrious in business," etc., and these are the only references to his work. One entry in the diary reads: "Had another evidence of the important truth that like will beget its like. I took a sign, which I had painted, to a storekeeper, and told him my price, but observed that I was afraid it was too much and if he thought so I would take less. The storekeeper paid me cheerfully, only manifesting a fear that I had charged too little. Ah! there is such a thing as dealing on Christian principles, there is such a thing as doing right and being happy in this world."

32

When he was old and could not work hard in his shop, he records "a difficulty and uneasiness in being so much of my time idle." Nevertheless, "he continued painting till the day before he died, when feeling himself very weak, he returned to the house, saying he believed that he had paid his last visit to the shop. The next morning his daughter observed 'she thought him better.' He replied he was better, he was comfortable, but requested they would not flatter themselves for he was going to die." He died in Newtown, August 23, 1849, and is buried there.

His paintings are owned by a number of private collectors, especially members of the Hicks family, and by the Friends' Home in Newtown, the Doylestown Museum, and the American Folk Art Gallery. The Hicks family owns a portrait of him painted by his cousin Thomas Hicks, the portrait painter, who began as an apprentice at coach painting in Edward Hicks' shop

*22 THE GRAVE OF WILLIAM PENN, 1847. *Oil on canvas.* H. 24″ W. 30″
By Edward Hicks. Inscribed on canvas: "The Grave of Wm. Penn at Jordans in England."
Inscribed on back of stretcher: "Painted by E. Hicks in his 68th year, For his friend Ann Drake." See No. 21

*23 THE TRUE CROSS, 1790–1800. *Oil on bed ticking.* H. 24 W. 34
Found near New Hope, Pennsylvania. Inscription reads: "Jesus saith. I thirst. So they put a spong full of vinegar upon a reed and gave him to drink."

*24 MANCHESTER VALLEY. *Oil on canvas.* H. 45″ W. 60″
By Joseph Pickett, 1848–1918. Signed: "Jos. Pickett Art. Manchester Valley, New Hope, Pa."
Joseph Pickett lived and died in New Hope, Pennsylvania. Like the rest of his family he was a carpenter and canal boat builder, and later in life he kept a little country grocery store on the banks of the Delaware Canal. The building is still standing and on its front wall, under a layer of stucco, is Pickett's first attempt at painting. At the top of the wall the stucco has peeled off, revealing the painted tops of trees. Pickett began to paint late in life. His ambition was to paint the history of his native town. He painted three large canvases, supposedly in the order named, *Washington Under the Council Tree*, now in the Newark Museum, *Manchester Valley*, in the present collection, and *Coryell's Ferry and Washington Taking Views* now in the Whitney Museum of American Art. These are the only oil paintings Pickett is known to have made, although one or two small sketches by him have been discovered. He used to exhibit his paintings in the window of his grocery store. In the year of his death he was persuaded by a resident of the artist colony at New Hope to send one of his paintings to the Pennsylvania Academy exhibition, where it is said to have received three jury votes, those of William L. Lathrop, Robert Henri and Robert Spencer. After Pickett's death his paintings were put up at auction, but as they brought only a dollar apiece his widow bought them in, and gave the *Manchester Valley* to the New Hope High School where it

hung for ten or twelve years. Relatives and neighbors of Pickett in New Hope remember little about him. New Hope artists who knew him say he was the typical American artisan, uneducated except in his trade. He was never taught even the rudiments of art, but invented his technique and his tools as he went along, spending long periods of time on each painting. He made his own brushes and used ordinary house paint, which he mixed with sand, earth, rocks and shells in an effort to imitate textures, an effort in which he succeeded remarkably well

25 OLD TENNENT CHURCH, *late eighteenth century.* *Oil on linen.* H. 8″ w. 10¼″
Found in Freehold, New Jersey. Old Tennent Church in Monmouth County, New Jersey, was built in 1751. An earlier building on the spot was built in 1731 by a congregation which moved from Old Scots Ground near Wickatunk, New Jersey. Near the church was fought the Battle of Monmouth in 1778, and the church was used as a hospital

*26 SOUTHERN SCENE, 1815–1830. *Oil on canvas.* H. 33″ w. 36″
Found in New York

*27 HUDSON RIVER SCENE, *about* 1870. *Oil on cardboard.* H. 19″ w. 24″
Found in Ulster County, New York

*28 PUBLIC BUILDING—NEW ENGLAND. *Over-mantle, oil on wood.* H. 30¾″ w. 35½″
Found in Massachusetts

29 WOMAN IN LANDSCAPE, 1800–1820. *Oil on wood.* H. 14″ w. 20″
Found in Boston

30 WHITE SAILS, *late nineteenth century.* *Oil on canvas.* H. 17″ w. 28¼′
By I. L. Emerson (signed). Found in Maine

PASTELS

31 CHILD WITH BLUE SASH, 1865. H. 28½″ w. 20½″
By Jonnie E. Berry (signed). Found in Woodstock, New York. Nothing is known about this artist

*32. "GEORGIE—QUITE TIRED," *about* 1850. H. 18½″ w. 14¼″
Found in New Hampshire. Taken from a Currier & Ives print

33 PROFILE OF BOY, *about* 1820. H. 16″ w. 12″
Found in Bridgeport, Connecticut

*34 PORTRAIT OF A MAN, *about* 1815.   H. 23½″ W. 19½″
Found in New Jersey. This and No. 35 by the same artist are said to be portraits of members of the Vanderveer family of Monmouth County, New Jersey. Two portraits of Newark citizens in the New Jersey Historical Society appear to have been done by the same artist. Another portrait in a New York collection, evidently by the same artist, is signed "H..C, 1819."

*35 WOMAN HOLDING BOOK, *about* 1815.   H. 23½″ W. 19½″
Found in New Jersey. See No. 34.

36 GIRL WITH ROSE, *about* 1810.   H. 24″ W. 18½″
Found in New York

*37 MOUNTAIN LANDSCAPE, *date undetermined*.   H. 14½″ W. 21½″
Found in Long Island, New York

WATERCOLORS

*38 MAN WITH WHITE STOCK, *about* 1830.   H. 19½″ W. 15¾″
Found in Bridgeport, Connecticut

39 PORTRAIT OF A WOMAN, 1810–1820.   H. 5″ W. 4″
Found in New York.   Pin-prick technique in collar and cap

*40 THE YORKE FAMILY AT HOME, 1837.   H. 10¾″ W. 14½″
Found in New York

41 MR. AND MRS. EBEN DAVIS, *about* 1840.   H. 13″ W. 15″
Found in Boston

42 WOMAN IN PROFILE, 1810–1820.   H. 4¾″ W. 3¼″
By E. C. P. (signed). Found in New York. This and No. 43 are a pair

43 MAN IN PROFILE, 1810–1820.   H. 4¾″ W. 3¼″
Probably by E. C. P. Found in New York

*44 GIRL IN BLUE WITH ORANGE FLOWERS, 1840–1850.   H. 11¼″ W. 7¼″
Found in Carlisle, Pennsylvania

45 "THE TO LOVERS, 1841."   H. 7½″ W. 5½″
Found in Providence, Rhode Island

*46 CHILDREN AND GOVERNESS, 1800-1810.   H. 14¾″ W. 17¾″
Found in Boston

47 THE GAY CAVALIER, *about* 1820.   H. 7½″ W. 11½″
By E. P. Davis (signed).   Found in Boston

*48 REBECCA AT THE WELL, 1800-1810.   H. 14½″ W. 18″
Found in Bridgeport, Connecticut

*49 MOSES IN THE BULRUSHES, *early nineteenth century. On silk.*   H. 21¼″ W. 17½″
Found near Wells, Maine

50 JOSEPH INTERPRETING PHARAOH'S DREAM.   H. 8¾″ W. 11¼″
Found near Ogunquit, Maine

51 JOSEPH INTRODUCING HIS BRETHREN.   H. 8¾″ W. 11¼″
Found near Ogunquit, Maine

52 MOURNING PICTURE—JOHN BARON, 1807.   H. 14¼″ W. 18¼″
Found in Bridgeport, Connecticut.   Inscription on tomb reads: "In memory of John Baron
who died—May 19, 1807, aged 23 years."

*53 "THE DEPARTURE OF LEATHER STOCKINGS."   H. 17¾″ W. 25¼″
Found in Greenwich, Connecticut. Subject taken from the writings of James Fenimore
Cooper

54 A VIEW OF ALBANY.   H. 9″ W. 12″
By E. B. Walker (signed).   Found in Waldoboro, Maine.   Nothing is known about this
artist

*55 "THE MONUMENT OF REV. J. HARVARD."   H. 9¼″ W. 13½″
By E. B. Walker (signed).   Found in Waldoboro, Maine

*56 "THE RESIDENCE OF GEN. WASHINGTON, MT. VERNON, VIR.," 1842.   H.
17½″ W. 21¼″
Found in Boston. Signed: "Painted by Susan Whitcomb at the Lit. Sci. Institution, Brandon,
Vt. 1842." The catalogue of the Literary Scientific Institution for 1842 lists Susan Whitcomb as a pupil. This painting was copied from an aquatint drawn by Alexander Robertson, engraved by Francis Jukes, and published by Robertson in New York and Jukes in
London in 1800

57 HARPER'S FERRY, VIRGINIA.   H. 21½″ W. 27″
Found in New Haven, Connecticut

58 HOUSE WITH WHITE FENCE.   H. 12¼″ W. 17″
Found in Bridgeport, Connecticut

59 THE DUCK POND, *about* 1820.   H. 5″ W. 6¾″
Found in Marblehead, Massachusetts

60 THE HOSPITAL.   H. 6¾″ W. 8¾″
Found in Boston

61 HOTEL WORCESTER, 1832.   H. 8¾″ W. 12¾″
By Emeline Morton (signed).   Found in Richmond, Virginia

*62 GLASS BOWL WITH FRUIT, *about* 1820.   H. 17″ W. 13¾″
Found in New Haven, Connecticut

*63 BASKET OF FRUIT, 1854.   H. 20½″ W. 28½″
Found in East Orange, New Jersey

64 STILL LIFE WITH WATERMELONS, *early nineteenth century*.   H. 17¾″ W. 21¼″
Found in Boston.   Design similar to that of velvet painting No. 81

65 YELLOW BOWL WITH FRUIT.   H. 9¾″ W. 17″
By Mary R. Wilson (signed on back of frame).   Found in Boston

*66 FRUIT IN YELLOW BASKET.   H. 9¾″ W. 12¾″
Found in Boston

67 FRUIT IN WHITE BASKET   H. 10¾″ W. 13¾″
Found in Boston

68 APPLE.   H. 5½″ W. 6½″
Found in York, Pennsylvania

69 PINEAPPLE.   H. 9½″ W. 7¾″
Found in Boston

70 FRUIT AND LEAVES.   H. 9¾″ W. 13″
Found in Boston

*71 WATCH AND FOB, 1829.   H. 8¼″ W. 6¼″
Inscribed: "George R. H. Slack's May 8th 1829."   Found in Washington, Connecticut

*72 HORSE WITH SADDLE.   H. 23¼″ W. 17″
Found in Bucks County, Pennsylvania. Pennsylvania German *fractur* technique (quill draw-ing and wash method)

*73 CRUCIFIXION, 1847.   H. 13¾″ W. 10¾″
Found in New York. Pennsylvania German *fractur* technique

*74 BIRTH CERTIFICATE OF MARIE PORTZLINE, June 11, 1820.   H. 13″ W. 16″
By Francis Portzline (signed). Inscribed: "Marie Portzline, daughter of Francis and Sabina Portzline, born June 11, 1820, in Chapman Township, Union County, Penn." Francis Portzline was a well-known maker of *fractur*, and many examples of his work have been found in Lancaster and Union Counties, Pennsylvania

75 BIRTH CERTIFICATE, 1798.   H. 10¼″ W. 7¾″
Found in Berks County, Pennsylvania. Pennsylvania German *fractur* technique

76 THE PEACEABLE KINGDOM.   H. 7¼″ W. 9¼″
Found in Lancaster County, Pennsylvania. Pennsylvania German *fractur* technique. Sub-ject taken from Isaiah XI, verses 6–7

77 PROMENADE.   H. 7½″ W. 9½″
Found in Long Island, New York. A Pennsylvania German artist's interpretation of the Orient, a curious mixture of Chinese and Persian influences, probably based on memories of pictures

78 BRIGHT BIRDS.   H. 10″ W. 7½″
Found at Ephrata, Pennsylvania. Pennsylvania German *fractur* technique

PAINTINGS ON VELVET

The period for velvet paintings is about 1800 to 1840. Most of the paintings in this collection date from the first half of this period. A few of them are signed and dated.

*79 STILL LIFE.   H. 14½″ W. 17½″
By Matilda A. Haviland (signed). Found in New York

*80 FRUIT ON TABLE.   H. 11½″ W. 15½″
Found in Boston

*81 STILL LIFE WITH WATERMELONS.   H. 17″ W. 22½″
Found in Boston

*82 FORMAL STILL LIFE. H. 14¾″ w. 15¾″
By Eleanor L. Coward (signed). Found in Freehold, New Jersey

83 BOWL OF FRUIT. H. 14½″ w. 20½″
Found in Boston

84 BOWL OF FRUIT. H. 14¼″ w. 20″
Found in Boston

85 THE BLUE BOWL. H. 16½″ w. 18½″
Found in Boston

86 BASKET OF FRUIT. H. 8½″ w. 8″
Found in Boston

*87 FRUIT, BIRD AND BUTTERFLY. H. 14″ w. 17¼″
Found in Boston

88 BASKET OF FRUIT. H. 5½″ w. 7¾″
Found in Boston

89 THE WICKER BASKET. H. 11¾″ w. 14¼″
Found in Boston

90 BASKET WITH SCROLL DESIGN. H. 5¼″ w. 8¾″
Signed H. N. Found in Boston

91 THE FULL BASKET. H. 11¼″ w. 14¼″
Found in Boston

92 THE FULL BASKET. H. 9¾″ w. 13½″
Found in Marblehead, Massachusetts

93 THE FULL BASKET. H. 12¼″ w. 13¾″
Found in Boston

94 BASKET OF FRUIT WITH BUTTERFLY. H. 11¼″ w. 15½″
Found in Greenwich, Connecticut

95 FRUIT ON BRANCH. H. 5½″ w. 6½″
Found in Boston

39

96 PEACHES, GRAPES AND STRAWBERRIES. H. 8" w. 8"
Found in Boston

97 PEACHES, GRAPES AND STRAWBERRIES. H. 5½" w. 6¾"
Found in Boston

*98 PEARS AND APPLES. H. 9" w. 13½"
Found in Long Island, New York

99 FLOWERS, BIRDS AND BUTTERFLIES, 1810-1820. H. 18½" w. 20½"
Possibly by Lydia Hosmer. Found near Concord, Massachusetts. A painting by Lydia
Hosmer in the Concord Antiquarian Society is almost identical with this one

100 BOWL OF FLOWERS. H. 12½" w. 15"
Found in Boston

101 BASKET OF FLOWERS. H. 14" w. 17"
Found in Philadelphia

102 FLOWERS IN BLUE BOWL. H. 15½" w. 18½"
Found in Boston

103 BRIGHT FLOWERS. H. 10" w. 12"
Found in Boston

104 PITCHER PLANT. H. 12¾" w. 11½"
Found in Boston

*105 PARROT. H. 22¼" w. 17¼"
Found in Bucks County, Pennsylvania

*106 MOURNING PICTURE—CLARK FAMILY, 1824. H. 17¼" w. 22"
Found in Boston. Inscriptions on the tombs read: "In memory of Clarissa M. Clark and
Caroline G. Clark who died Aug. 21, 1824, aged 9 months." "In memory of Samuel N.
Clark who died Nov. 2, 1811, aged 19 months."

107 MOURNING PICTURE—ELIZA H. OSGOOD, 1832. H. 17¼" w. 20¾"
Found in Bucks County, Pennsylvania. Inscription on the tomb reads: "Sacred to the
memory of Eliza H. Osgood who died Oct. 7, 1832, aged 18 months."

"Our Heavenly Father marked the flower
Saw 'twas to fair to stay.
And in a few few transient hours
He summon'd her away."

*108 RUTH AND NAOMI. H. 20½" w. 25½"
Found in New York

109 COURTING, 1825. H. 12" w. 15¾"
By Mary Ann Kimball (signed). Found in Bucks County, Pennsylvania

110 SHEPHERDESS. H. 9½" w. 7¾"
Found in Marblehead, Massachusetts

111 SILHOUETTES, *about* 1815. H. 4¼" w. 6"
Found in Boston

PAINTINGS ON GLASS

*112 ELISABETH, *about* 1820. H. 8¾" w. 6¾"
Pennsylvania German. Found in Hagerstown, Maryland

113 MELON, PLUMS AND GRAPES. H. 6¾" w. 8½"
Found in Boston

114 WHEAT STACK. H. 10" w. 7¾"
Pennsylvania German. Found in Bucks County, Pennsylvania

115 THE GOVERNMENT HOUSE, BOWLING GREEN, NEW YORK. *Engraving and oil painting on glass.* H. 9½" w. 12½"
Found in Sellersville, Pennsylvania

*116 "THE BATTLE BETWEEN THE CONSTITUTION AND GUERIERE, 19 AUG.
1812." H. 17½" w. 19¼"
By E. Webb (signed). Found in Massachusetts

*117 URN OF ROSES WITH BUTTERFLIES. *Tinsel and oil painting on glass.* H. 21½"
w. 17½"
Found in Ridgefield, Connecticut

DESIGN GROUP
One design carried out in five different media.

118 PAINTING ON VELVET. H. 12¼" w. 9½"
Found in Boston

119 WATERCOLOR.   H. 14″   W. 11″
Found in Boston

120 TINSEL AND OIL PAINTING ON GLASS.   H. 15¾″   W. 11¾″
Found in Maine

121 LITHOGRAPH WITH WATERCOLOR.   H. 14″   W. 9¾″
Found in Marblehead, Massachusetts

122 LITHOGRAPH AND PENCIL DRAWING.   H. 13¾″   W. 9¾″
Found in Maine

WOOD SCULPTURE

*123 MINNEHAHA, *ship's figurehead, polychromed.*   H. 75″
Found in the West Indies by the late Max Williams

*124 BUST OF GIRL, *ship's figurehead, painted.*   H. 28″
Found in Bridgeport, Connecticut. Said to be from a boat which sailed on Long Island Sound

*125 INDIAN, *cigar store figure.*   H. 50½″
Found near Stockbridge, Massachusetts

*126 TRAPPER INDIAN, *cigar store figure, painted.*   H. 42¾″
Found near Stockbridge, Massachusetts

*127 HENRY WARD BEECHER, 1850–1860.   H. 21″
Said to have been carved by a farmer named Corbin at Centerville, Indiana, during a visit which Beecher made to Corbin's home

128 GEORGE WASHINGTON, *polychromed.*   H. 11¾″
Pennsylvania German. Found in Wilmington, Delaware

*129 SEATED WOMAN, *polychromed.*   H. 12″
Pennsylvania German.   Found near Ephrata, Pennsylvania

*130 ROOSTER, *polychromed.*   H. 10½″
Found in New York. Stylized rooster of the type known as "Pennsylvania pine"

131 EAGLE, *painted.*   H. 6½″ W. 25½″   (Reproduced on front cover)
By John Bellamy, 1836–1914. Found in Maine. Bellamy lived at Kittery Point, Maine, and was the last of the famous wood-carvers of that section. During the Civil War he worked at the Portsmouth Navy Yard, carving figureheads for warships. He is best known for his eagles, large ones used as figureheads, and small ones of this type to be placed over doorways on ships and public buildings

*132 EAGLE.   H. 68″ *(with base)*
Said to have been a sign for The Eagle Tavern in Pawtucket, Rhode Island.   Found in Providence

133 EAGLE, *black and white.   Probably a flagpole top.*   H. 33¾″ *(with base)*
Found in Hartford, Connecticut

*134 EAGLE, *polychromed.*   H. 15½″ *Wing Spread* 32″
Found in Carlisle, Pennsylvania. Type known as Schimmel carving. Schimmel was a Pennsylvania German of uncertain date, whose work was in the tradition of German peasant art

135 HEAD OF A BIRD.   L. 20¼″
Found near Rockland, Maine. Said to represent the mythical roc. Originally used as a billet-head of a ship

*136 STYLIZED ROOSTER, *weather-vane, polychromed.*   H. 14½″
Found near Portsmouth, New Hampshire

137 ROOSTER, *weather-vane, painted.*   H. 14″
Found in Pottstown, Pennsylvania

138 WOMAN, *pipe figure.*   H. 8½″
Found near Pottstown, Pennsylvania.   The hat forms the bowl of the pipe

*139 PRIMITIVE HORSE.   H. 14″ L. 21¾″
Found in Germantown, Pennsylvania

*140 TOY HORSE, *painted.*   H. 11¾″ L. 13¼″
Pennsylvania German.   Found in Carlisle, Pennsylvania

141 SPOTTED HORSE, *toy.*   H. 5¾″ L. 5½″
Pennsylvania German.   Found in Carlisle, Pennsylvania

142 HORSE WITH FLOWING TAIL, *toy.*   H. 14½″
Found at Buzzard's Bay, Massachusetts

43

*143 PIGEON, *polychromed.* H. 11½″
Pennsylvania German. Found in Pottstown, Pennsylvania

144 BIRD, *toy.* H. 5½″
Pennsylvania German. Found in Carlisle, Pennsylvania

*145 LOON, *decoy, painted.* H. 11½″
Probably Pennsylvania German. Found in Teaneck, New Jersey

146 LOON WITH SILVER TAIL. H. 5½″
Found in Ephrata, Pennsylvania

147 PAIR OF DUCKS, *miniature decoys.* L. 4½″ *and* 5″
Found near Barnegat Bay, New Jersey

SCULPTURE IN METAL

*148 GEORGE WASHINGTON, *lawn figure.* H. 46½″
Found in Connecticut

*149 FORMAL HORSE, *weather-vane.* *Cast iron.* H. 18″ L. 20″
Found in Boston. Another horse cast from the same mold has been found near Boston

150 HORSE WITH FLOWING TAIL, *weather-vane.* *Cast and stamped metal.* H. 18″
L. 24¼″
Found in Salem, Massachusetts

*151 HORSE AND SULKY, *weather-vane.* *Cast iron and stamped metal.* H. 17½″ L. 37″
Found in Boston. Horse is copied from a Currier & Ives print of the racehorse Ethan Allen

152 ROOSTER, *weather-vane, about* 1810. *Stamped and hammered metal.* H. 34¼″
Originally on a building owned by the St. Nicholas Society in New York

*153 FORMAL ROOSTER, *weather-vane.* *Cast iron with cut-out tail.* H. 23½″
Found in Boston

154 ROOSTER, *weather-vane.* *Cast metal with cut-out tail.* H. 12¾
Found on Cape Cod, Massachusetts

*155 PHEASANT, *weather-vane.* *Iron cut-out.* L. 30¾″
Found at Monterey, Pennsylvania

156 BIRD, *weather-vane.   Stamped and hammered copper.*   H. 17½″
Found in Sugartown, Pennsylvania

*157 COW, *weather-vane.   Cast and stamped copper.*   H. 16¾″ L. 28″
Found in Boston

*158 SHEEP, *weather-vane. Stamped, hammered and cast metal.*   H. 20½″ L. 31″
Found in Bucks County, Pennsylvania

*159 THE SWARM OF BEES, *stove plate, middle eighteenth century.*   Cast iron.   H. 23½″
w. 27¾″
Pennsylvania German.   Found in Shenandoah County, Virginia

*160 THE PEACEABLE KINGDOM, *stove plate, middle eighteenth century.*   Cast iron.
H. 20½″ w. 22¼″
Pennsylvania German. Found in Shenandoah County, Virginia

161 FIRE INSURANCE EMBLEM, 1860.   *Cast iron.*   H. 9⅝″ w. 11⅜″
Fire-mark of the United Firemen's Insurance Company of Philadelphia, founded in 1860

162 PATTERN GROUP, *fifteen designs for cookie molds, cut out of metal.*
Found in Lancaster County, Pennsylvania

PLASTER ORNAMENTS

*163 BUST OF A MAN, *early nineteenth century.*   H. 14″
Found in Lancaster County, Pennsylvania

164 GIRL IN BLOOMER COSTUME, 1851–1853.   H. 10½″
Found in Lancaster County, Pennsylvania.   Taken from a Currier & Ives print

165 ANGEL.   H. 11¼″
Found in Bucks County, Pennsylvania

166 CHILD WITH BIRD.   H. 12″
Found in Lancaster County, Pennsylvania

*167 LADY, *candleholder.*   H. 16¼″
Found in Lancaster County, Pennsylvania

168 CHILD.   H. 4¼″
Found in Bucks County, Pennsylvania

169 WOMAN ON HORSE.   H. 7″
Found on Cape Cod, Massachusetts

170 PAIR OF ROOSTERS.   H. 12¼″
Found in Bucks County, Pennsylvania

*171 DOG.   H. 7½″
Found in Lancaster County, Pennsylvania

*172 DEER, 1883.   H. 10¾″
Found in Bucks County, Pennsylvania

173 DOVE, *bank*.   H. 7¾″
Found in Bucks County, Pennsylvania

174 CAT.   H. 15¼″
Found in New York

175 SQUIRREL.   H. 6½″
Found in Lancaster County, Pennsylvania

BIBLIOGRAPHY

BOOKS

ADAMS, J. T., *Provincial Society, 1690–1763*. The Macmillan Company, New York, 1927. Background of early folk art

ALLEN, E. B., *Early American Wall Paintings*. Yale University Press, New Haven, Conn., 1926. A study of wall paintings in houses in New England, New York and the South from 1710 to 1850

ALLEN, F. H. (editor), *Journal of Amasa Hewins*. The Boston Athenaeum, 1931. Journal of a Boston portrait painter's visit to Italy

APPERSON, G. L., *The Social History of Smoking*. G. P. Putnam's Sons, New York, 1916. English; includes a chapter on tobacconists' signs

BARKER, VIRGIL, *A Critical Introduction to American Painting*. Whitney Museum of American Art, New York, 1931. Contains brief references to folk art and a list of twenty-one folk painters

BEARD, C. A. and M. R., *The Rise of American Civilization;* 2 vols. The Macmillan Company, New York, 1930. Social, economic and political background

BISHOP, J. L., *A History of American Manufactures;* 2 vols. Edward Young and Company, Philadelphia, 1864. Origins of American manufactures and methods, and story of early ship-builders, iron-founders, etc.

BITTINGER, L. F., *The Germans in Colonial Times*. J. B. Lippincott Company, Philadelphia, 1901. Background of the Pennsylvania German types of folk art

BOLTON, C. K., *The Founders;* 3 vols. The Boston Athenaeum, 1919. Portraits of persons born abroad who came to the colonies before 1701. Contains also a list of portraits of more than four hundred persons born in the colonies before 1701

BOWLES, E. S., *About Antiques*. J. B. Lippincott Company, Philadelphia, 1929. Arts and crafts

BUCKS COUNTY HISTORICAL SOCIETY, *Collection of Papers Read Before the* . . . vols. 1–6, 1909–1932. Published for the Society by Fackenthal Publication Fund, 1917. Papers on Pennsylvania German folk arts and crafts

BURROUGHS, P. H., *Southern Antiques*. Garrett and Massie, Inc., Richmond, Va., 1931. Craftsmen, particularly wood-carvers and joiners, working in the South

CLARK, A. H., *The Clipper Ship Era*. G. P. Putnam's Sons, New York, 1910

Cousins, Frank and P. M. Riley, *The Wood-carver of Salem*. Little Brown and Company, Boston, 1916. Life of Samuel McIntire

Crouse, Russel, *Mr. Currier and Mr. Ives*. Doubleday, Doran and Company, Garden City, N. Y., 1930. Notes on the subjects of popular art in the nineteenth century

Currier, J. J., *History of Newburyport, Massachusetts;* 2 vols. Published by the Author, Newburyport, 1906–09. Contains a good account of "Lord" Timothy Dexter

Dow, G. F., *The Arts and Crafts in New England, 1704–1775*. The Wayside Press, Topsfield, Mass., 1927. Gleanings from Boston newspapers relating to eighteenth century American artists and craftsmen

Dunlap, William, *History of the Rise and Progress of the Arts of Design in the United States;* 3 vols. C. E. Goodspeed and Company, Boston, 1918. Lives and methods of early American artists

Dyer, W. A., *Creators of Decorative Styles*. Doubleday, Page and Company, Garden City, N. Y., 1917. Sources of early American styles

———— *Early American Craftsmen*. The Century Company, New York, 1915. Leading exponents of early American craft, some of whose work may be considered fine art

Earle, A. M., *Two Centuries of Costume in America;* 2 vols. The Macmillan Company, New York, 1910. American costume with particular reference to the costumes in old portraits

Eberlein, H. D. and Abbot McClure, *The Practical Book of American Antiques*. J. B. Lippincott Company, Philadelphia, 1927. The work of early American craftsmen

Faust, A. B., *The German Element in the United States;* vol. 2. The Houghton Mifflin Company, Boston, 1909

Fish, C. R., *The Rise of the Common Man, 1830–1850*. The Macmillan Company, New York, 1927. Social and political background of early nineteenth century folk art

Foote, H. W., *Robert Feke*. Harvard University Press, Cambridge, Mass., 1930. Notes on beginnings of art in the American colonies in early chapters

Forbes, H. M., *Gravestones of Early New England and the Men Who Made Them, 1653–1800*. The Houghton Mifflin Company, Boston, 1927. Early stone-carvers of New England

Gillingham, H. E., *American Fire-marks*. Privately printed, Philadelphia, 1914

Guild, L. Van A., *The Geography of American Antiques*. Doubleday, Doran and Company, Garden City, N. Y., 1931. Carvers, joiners and builders

HICKS, EDWARD, *Memoirs of the Life and Religious Labors of E. Hicks. Written by Himself.* Merrihew and Thompson, Philadelphia, 1851. The autobiography of a folk artist

LAUGHTON, L. G. C., *Old Ship, Figureheads and Sterns.* Halton and T. Smith, Ltd., London, 1925. An account of ships' carvings of all ages, beautifully illustrated

LESLIE, R. C., *Old Sea Wings, Ways and Words, in the Days of Oak and Hemp.* Chapman & Hall, Ltd., London, 1890. Two chapters on the history of figureheads

McCLELLAN, ELIZABETH, *Historic Dress in America;* 2 vols. George W. Jacobs & Company, Philadelphia, 1910. Identification of costumes in American portraits

McKAY, R. C., *Some Famous Sailing Ships and Their Builder, Donald McKay.* G. P. Putnam's Sons, New York, 1928

MARQUAND, J. P., *Lord Timothy Dexter of Newburyport, Massachusetts.* Minton, Balch and Company, New York, 1925. The life of a celebrated American eccentric who had a forest of folk sculptures at his estate in Newburyport

MERCER, H. C., *The Bible in Iron.* Bucks County Historical Society, Doylestown, Pa., 1914. Standard book on Pennsylvania German stove plates

———— *The Survival of the Medieval Art of Illuminative Writing Among the Pennsylvania Germans.* Bucks County Historical Society, Doylestown, Pa., (Contribution to American History, no. 2), 1898. Source book on the art of the *fractur* makers

MORGAN, J. H., *Early American Painters.* The New York Historical Society, 1921

PENNSYLVANIA-GERMAN SOCIETY, *Proceedings and Addresses;* vols. 1–33. Published by the Society, Lancaster, Pa., 1892–1923. Vol. 10 gives a detailed account of the life of the Pennsylvania Germans

PETERS, H. T., *America on Stone.* Doubleday, Doran and Company, Garden City, N. Y., 1931. A study of popular lithographs and their makers, other than Currier & Ives

———— *Currier & Ives, Printmakers to the American People;* 2 vols. Doubleday, Doran and Company, Garden City, N. Y., 1929–31

PRICE, J. M., *Dame Fashion.* Sampson Low, Marston and Company, London, 1912. American costume in relation to the costume of Europe

SANBORN, KATE, *Hunting Indians in a Taxicab.* Richard G. Badger, Boston, 1911. Cigar store figures

SHERMAN, F. F., *Early American Painting*. The Century Company, New York, 1932

———— *Early American Portraiture*. Privately printed, New York, 1930

SIZER, THEODORE, *Aspects of the Social History of America*, by Theodore Sizer, A. C. McLaughlin, D. R. Fox and H. S. Canby. The University of North Carolina Press, Chapel Hill, N. C., 1931

STOKES, I. N. P. and D. C. HASKELL, *American Historical Prints*, Early Views of American Cities, etc. New York Public Library, 1932.

SWANK, J. M., *The History and Manufacture of Iron in All Ages*. Published by the Author, Philadelphia, 1884. Descriptions of many early American furnaces

TUCKERMAN, H. T., *Book of the Artists*. G. P. Putnam and Son, New York, 1867. Artists' biographies

STANARD, M. N., *Colonial Virginia, Its People and Customs*. J. B. Lippincott Co., Philadelphia, 1917

URBINO, LEVINA, *Art Recreations*. S. W. Tilton and Company, Boston. This book appears to have gone through several editions between 1859 and 1884. Gives directions for painting on velvet, silk and glass, and for various other kinds of art work popular in the Victorian era

WARWICK, EDWARD and H. C. PITZ, *Early American Costume*. The Century Company, New York, 1929. American costume with particular reference to the costumes in old portraits

WEYGANDT, CORNELIUS, *The Red Hills*. University of Pennsylvania Press, Philadelphia, 1929. Background of the arts and crafts of the Pennsylvania "country Dutch"

WRIGHT, RICHARDSON, *Hawkers and Walkers in Early America*. J. B. Lippincott Company, Philadelphia, 1927. Notes on peddlers and itinerants who distributed the products of American craftsmen. Chapter IX on the artist as an itinerant

PERIODICALS

ALLEN, E. B., Old American Weather Vanes. *International Studio*, LXXX, Mar. 1925, pp. 450–53

ANONYMOUS, Add Americana: The Decoy. *Fortune*, VI, Aug. 1932, pp. 38–42. Article on a collection of wild fowl decoys

BARKER, VIRGIL, Notes on the Exhibitions. *The Arts*, V, Mar. 1924, pp. 160–61. Whitney Studio Club show of American primitives

BRANSCOMBE, HENRY, Early American Wood Sculpture. *International Studio*, LXXXVIII, Oct. 1927, pp. 61–64

BROOK, ALEXANDER, Portrait Painters Incognito. *Charm*, III, Feb. 1925, pp. 38–39 and 89. Article on portrait limners

BROWN, M. L., John Welsh, Carver. *Antiques*, IX, Jan. 1926, p. 28

CAHILL, HOLGER, American Folk Art. *American Mercury*, XXIV, Sept. 1931, pp. 39–46

———— Folk Art—Its Place in the American Tradition. *Parnassus*, IV, Mar. 1932, pp. 1–4

CIOLKOWSKA, MURIEL, American Primitives. *Artwork*, III, Sept.–Nov. 1927

EBERLEIN, H. D., What Early America Had on Its Walls. *International Studio*, LXXXVIII, Sept. 1927, pp. 52–56

EGLINGTON, GUY, Art and Other Things. *International Studio*, LXXX, Feb. 1925, pp. 418–19. Notes on an exhibition of American primitives at the Dudensing Gallery, New York

FORBES, H. M., Early Portrait Sculpture in New England. *Old-Time New England*, XVIII, Apr. 1929, pp. 159–73

FRASER, E. S., Some Colonial and Early American Decorative Floors. *Antiques*, XIX, Apr. 1931, pp. 296–301

GILLIAMS, E. L., A Philadelphia Sculptor: William Rush. *Lippincott's Magazine*, LII, Aug. 1893, pp. 249–53

GILLINGHAM, H. E., The Fascinating Fire-mark. *Antiques*, IV, Dec. 1923, pp. 277–80

GOODRICH, LLOYD, Current Exhibitions. *The Arts*, VII, Jan. 1925, pp. 46–47. Notes on an exhibition of American primitives at the Dudensing Gallery, New York

GOULD, MR. and MRS. G. G., Eighteenth Century Cottage Ornaments. *House and Garden*, LVII, May 1930, pp. 124, 142–48

———— Nadelman Ship Figureheads. *International Studio*, XCIV, Sept. 1929, pp. 51–53

———— Plaster Ornaments for Collectors. *House and Garden*, LVI, Aug. 1929, pp. 84, 122

HARVARD SOCIETY FOR CONTEMPORARY ART, Introduction to *Catalogue of Exhibit of American Folk Painting*, Oct. 15–31, 1930

JESSUP, L. F., The Tobacconists' Tribe of Treen. *Antiques*, XVIII, Sept. 1930, pp. 232–35. Article on cigar store Indians

JORDAN, W., William Rush, Earliest Native-born American Sculptor. *Art and Archaeology*, XI, June 1921, pp. 245–47

KARR, LOUISE, Paintings on Velvet. *Antiques*, XX, Sept. 1931, pp. 162–65

———— Old Westwood Murals. *Antiques*, IX, Apr. 1926, pp. 231–36

KEYES, H. E., Some American Primitives. *Antiques*, XII, Aug. 1927, pp. 118–22

KIMBALL, FISKE, Beginnings of Sculpture in Colonial America. *Art and Archaeology*, VIII, June 1919, pp. 185–89

McKEARIN, H. A., Schimmel, Carver of a Menagerie. *New York Sun*, Nov. 16, 1929, p. 35, cols. 1–3

METROPOLITAN MUSEUM OF ART, Some Carved Figures by Samuel McIntire. *Bulletin*, XVIII, Aug. 1923, pp. 194–96

MORRISON, J. L., Passing of the Wooden Indian. *Scribner's Magazine*, LXXXIV, Oct. 1928, pp. 393–405

NELSON, MRS. H. C., Early American Primitives. *International Studio*, LXXX, Mar. 1925, pp. 450–59

NEWARK MUSEUM, *American Folk Sculpture*. Catalogue by Holger Cahill and Elinor Robinson of an exhibit of the work of eighteenth and nineteenth century craftsmen, Oct. 20, 1931 to Jan. 31, 1932

———— *American Primitives*. Catalogue by Holger Cahill and Elinor Robinson of an exhibit of the paintings of nineteenth century folk artists, Nov. 4, 1930 to Feb. 1, 1931

PENNSYLVANIA MUSEUM, Cast Iron stoves of the Pennsylvania Germans. *Bulletin*, XIII, Apr. 1915, pp. 19–22

SNOW, J. D. S., King *versus* Ellsworth. *Antiques*, XXI, Mar. 1932, pp. 118–21. Notes on the lives and methods of itinerant portrait painters

STOW, C. M., A Portrait in Iron. *The Antiquarian*, XIV, June 1930, pp. 29–31

WATSON, E. S., Figureheads of the Old Square-riggers; explanatory texts by Victoria Hayward. *Century*, XCII, Aug. 1916, pp. 566–73. A set of photographs with text

WEITENKAMPF, F. W., Lo, the Wooden Indian. *New York Times*, Aug. 3, 1890, p. 13, col. 1

WILSON, ROBERT, Art and Artists in Provincial South Carolina. *Charleston South Carolina Yearbook*, 1899, appendix, pp. 137–147

WORCESTER MUSEUM, Madam Freake and Baby Mary, by Raymond Henniker-Heaton. *Bulletin*, XIV, Oct. 1923, pp. 62–65

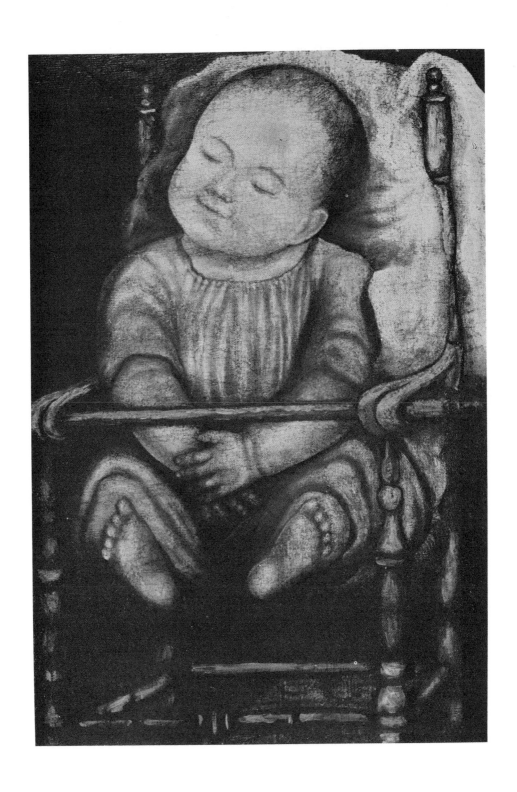

1 BABY IN RED HIGH CHAIR, *about* 1790. *Oil on canvas*

2 CHILD WITH DOG, *about* 1800.   *Oil on canvas*

3 THE BLUE BOY, *about 1830. Oil on canvas*

4 THE GIRL IN WHITE, *about* 1830. *Oil on canvas*

5 HELEN EDDY, *about 1840.* *Oil on canvas*

6 CHILD WITH WOODPECKER, *about 1840.* *Oil on canvas*

10 THREE CHILDREN, *about* 1830. *Oil on wood*

11 GIRL ON BALCONY, 1840–1850.   *Oil on canvas*

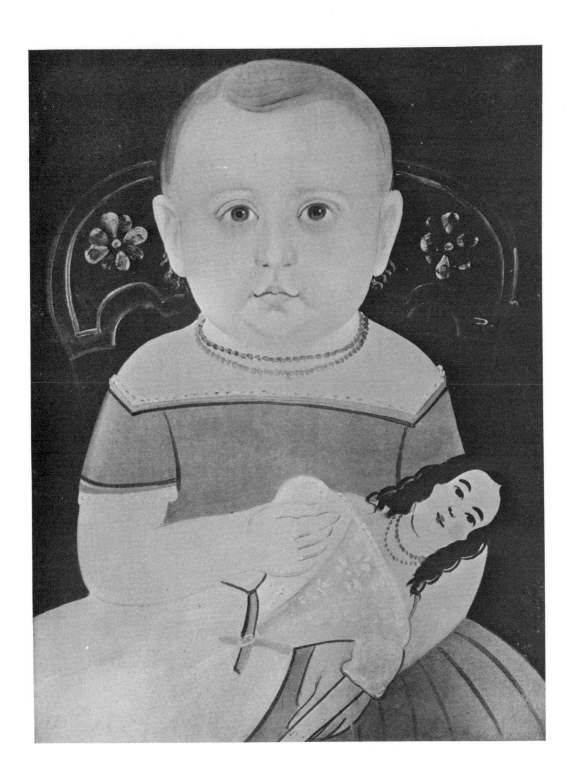

12 BABY WITH DOLL, 1840–1850. *Oil on canvas*

14 MR. HARRISON, *about 1815. Oil on wood*

15 MRS. HARRISON, *about 1815.* *Oil on wood*

18 WASHINGTON AND LAFAYETTE AT THE BATTLE OF THE BRANDYWINE.
Late eighteenth century.   Oil on canvas

19 POCAHONTAS SAVING CAPTAIN JOHN SMITH, *date undetermined.* *Oil on canvas*

20 THE CAPTURE OF MAJOR ANDRÉ, *exact date undetermined.*   *Oil on canvas*

21 THE PEACEABLE KINGDOM, *about 1833.* *Oil on canvas*

22 THE GRAVE OF WILLIAM PENN, 1847. *Oil on canvas*

23 THE TRUE CROSS, 1790–1800. *Oil on bed ticking*

24 MANCHESTER VALLEY. *Oil on canvas*

26 SOUTHERN SCENE, 1815–1830. *Oil on canvas*

27 HUDSON RIVER SCENE, *about 1870.* *Oil on cardboard*

28 PUBLIC BUILDING—NEW ENGLAND. *Over-mantle, oil on wood*

32 "GEORGIE—QUITE TIRED," *about 1850.* *Pastel*

34 PORTRAIT OF A MAN, *about 1815.* *Pastel*

35 WOMAN HOLDING BOOK, *about 1815.* *Pastel*

37 MOUNTAIN LANDSCAPE, *date undetermined.* *Pastel*

38 MAN WITH WHITE STOCK, *about 1830.* *Watercolor*

40 THE YORKE FAMILY AT HOME, 1837. *Watercolor*

44 GIRL IN BLUE WITH ORANGE FLOWERS, 1840–1850. *Watercolor*

46 CHILDREN AND GOVERNESS, 1800–1810. *Watercolor*

48 REBECCA AT THE WELL, 1800–1810. *Watercolor*

49 MOSES IN THE BULRUSHES, *early nineteenth century. Watercolor on silk*

53 "THE DEPARTURE OF LEATHER STOCKINGS." *Watercolor*

55 "THE MONUMENT OF REV. J. HARVARD." *Watercolor*

56 "THE RESIDENCE OF GEN. WASHINGTON, MT. VERNON, VIR.," 1842.   *Watercolor*

62 GLASS BOWL WITH FRUIT, *about* 1820.　　*Watercolor*

63 BASKET OF FRUIT, 1854. *Watercolor*

66 FRUIT IN YELLOW BASKET. *Watercolor*

71 WATCH AND FOB, 1829. *Watercolor*

72 HORSE WITH SADDLE. *Quill drawing and watercolor*

73 CRUCIFIXION, 1847. *Fractur*

74 BIRTH CERTIFICATE OF MARIE PORTZLINE, June 11, 1820.   *Fractur*

79 STILL LIFE.   *Velvet painting*

80 FRUIT ON TABLE.   *Velvet painting*

81 STILL LIFE WITH WATERMELONS.   *Velvet painting*

82 FORMAL STILL LIFE. *Velvet painting*

87 FRUIT, BIRD AND BUTTERFLY.   *Velvet painting*

98 PEARS AND APPLES. *Velvet painting*

105 PARROT. *Velvet painting*

106 MOURNING PICTURE—CLARK FAMILY, 1824. *Velvet painting*

108 RUTH AND NAOMI. *Velvet painting*

112 ELISABETH, *about 1820.* *Painting on glass*

116 "THE BATTLE BETWEEN THE CONSTITUTION AND GUERIERE, 19 AUG. 1812."
Painting on glass

117 URN OF ROSES WITH BUTTERFLIES.   *Tinsel and oil painting on glass*

123 MINNEHAHA, *ship's figurehead, polychromed*

124 BUST OF GIRL, *ship's figurehead, painted*

125 INDIAN, *cigar store figure*

126 TRAPPER INDIAN, *cigar store figure, painted*

127 HENRY WARD BEECHER, 1850–1860. *Wood sculpture*

129 SEATED WOMAN. *Wood sculpture, polychromed*

130 ROOSTER. *Wood sculpture, polychromed*

132 EAGLE. *Wood sculpture*

134 EAGLE. *Wood sculpture, polychromed*

136 STYLIZED ROOSTER, *weather-vane, polychromed*

139 PRIMITIVE HORSE.   *Wood sculpture*

140 TOY HORSE. *Wood sculpture, painted*

143 PIGEON. *Wood sculpture, polychromed*

145 LOON. *Wood sculpture, painted*

148 GEORGE WASHINGTON, *lawn figure.* Metal

149 FORMAL HORSE, *weather-vane.* *Cast iron*

151 HORSE AND SULKY, *weather-vane.*   *Cast iron and stamped metal*

153 FORMAL ROOSTER, *weather-vane.* *Cast iron with cut-out tail*

155 PHEASANT, *weather-vane.* Iron cut-out

157 COW, *weather-vane.   Cast and stamped copper*

158 SHEEP, *weather-vane.* *Stamped, hammered and cast metal*

159 THE SWARM OF BEES, *stove plate, middle eighteenth century.   Cast iron*

160 THE PEACEABLE
KINGDOM, *stove plate,*
middle eighteenth century.
Cast iron

163 BUST OF A MAN, *early nineteenth century.   Plaster*

167 LADY, *candleholder. Plaster*

171 DOG. *Plaster*

172 DEER, 1883. *Plaster*

FIFTEEN HUNDRED COPIES OF THIS CATAOLG WERE
PRINTED FOR THE TRUSTEES OF THE MUSEUM OF
MODERN ART, NEW YORK, BY PLANDOME PRESS,
NEW YORK, NOVEMBER, NINETEEN THIRTY-TWO